AHAM DA ASMI

(BELOVED, I AM DA)

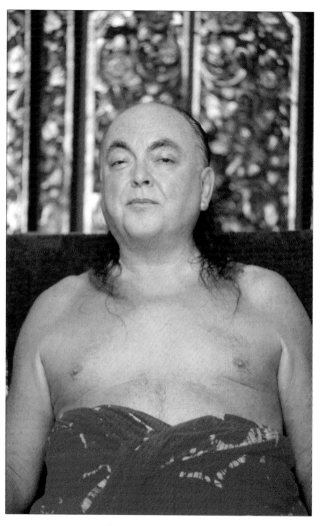

The Divine World-Teacher,
RUCHIRA AVATAR ADI DA SAMRAJ
Adidam Samrajashram (Naitauba), Fiji, 1998

AHAM DA ASMI
(BELOVED, I <u>AM</u> DA)

The Five Books Of
The Heart Of The Adidam Revelation

BOOK ONE

The "Late-Time" Avataric Revelation
Of The True and Spiritual Divine Person
(The egoless Personal Presence Of Reality and Truth,
Which <u>Is</u> The Only <u>Real</u> God)

By
The Divine World-Teacher,
RUCHIRA AVATAR
ADI DA SAMRAJ

THE DAWN HORSE PRESS
MIDDLETOWN, CALIFORNIA

NOTE TO THE READER

All who study Adidam (the Way of the Heart) or take up its practice should remember that they are responding to a Call to become responsible for themselves. They should understand that they, not Avatar Adi Da Samraj or others, are responsible for any decision they may make or action they take in the course of their lives of study or practice.

The devotional, Spiritual, functional, practical, relational, cultural, and formal community practices and disciplines referred to in this book are appropriate and natural practices that are voluntarily and progressively adopted by each student-novice and member of Adidam and adapted to his or her personal circumstance. Although anyone may find them useful and beneficial, they are not presented as advice or recommendations to the general reader or to anyone who is not a student-novice or a member of Adidam. And nothing in this book is intended as a diagnosis, prescription, or recommended treatment or cure for any specific "problem", whether medical, emotional, psychological, social, or Spiritual. One should apply a particular program of treatment, prevention, cure, or general health only in consultation with a licensed physician or other qualified professional.

CONTENTS

AHAM DA ASMI
(BELOVED, I <u>AM</u> DA)
65

FIRST WORD
Do Not Misunderstand <u>Me</u>—
I Am <u>Not</u> "Within" <u>you</u>, but you <u>Are</u> In <u>Me</u>, and
I Am <u>Not</u> a Mere "Man" in the "Middle" of Mankind,
but All of Mankind Is Surrounded,
and Pervaded, and Blessed By <u>Me</u>
67

PART ONE
Aham Da Asmi
(Beloved, I <u>Am</u> Da)
93

RUCHIRA AVATAR ADI DA SAMRAJ
Adidam Samrajashram (Naitauba), Fiji, 1997

The Divine Emergence of
The Ruchira Avatar,
Adi Da Samraj

The Realizer, the Revealer, and the Revelation
of the Divine and All-Completing Seventh Stage of Life

by
Carolyn Lee, Ph.D.

ham Da Asmi proclaims a Revelation of the Divine that surpasses anything that has ever been known in the conditionally manifested worlds. The Appearance here, in human Form, of the Supreme Giver, Ruchira Avatar Adi Da Samraj, is that Revelation, the Revelation of God Incarnate—Come to Bless and Awaken all beings in all realms to the All-Surpassing Truth and "Brightness"[1] of the Divine Reality. Ruchira Avatar Adi Da is the Promised God-Man. His Coming is the Love-Response of the Divine, in Person, to eons of prayer and longing, on the part of beings everywhere, to be restored to the Heart of Real God.[2]

The Appearance of the Ruchira Avatar, Adi Da Samraj, truly is <u>the</u> Great Event of history. It is the Event that Reveals the real meaning of the entire past, and the Great Purpose of all future time. His Avataric Incarnation[3] is the fruition of an infinitely vast Divine Process, originating

Carolyn Lee is a formal renunciate practitioner of the Way of Adidam living at Adidam Samrajashram (Fiji), the Great Island-Hermitage of the Ruchira Avatar, Adi Da Samraj.

Notes for this Introduction can be found on pp. 49-54.

before time and space itself, and developing throughout the Cosmic domain in response to the desperate prayers of beings everywhere, suffering the pain of apparent separation from Real God. In that unspeakable sweep of time, there have been unique beings who, through great struggle and sacrifice, made "windows" to the Divine for others. They gave Teachings and practices, were worshipped and honored, and have become the source of the entire human tradition of religion and Spirituality. Again and again, it has seemed to those alive in a particular time and place that the revelation was complete, the salvation perfect, the enlightenment given.

Even so, there has remained a thread of prophecy in all the great Spiritual traditions foretelling One yet to Appear, One Who must Come in the darkest time of humanity, when the world is at its worst, and bring to completion all the revelations of the past. Christians await the second coming of Jesus; Muslims, the Mahdhi (the last prophet); Buddhists, Maitreya (the coming Buddha); and Hindus, the Kalki Avatar (the final Avatar of Vishnu). Even as recently as February 1939, a celebrated Indian Adept, Upasani Baba, prophesied the imminent appearance of a Western-born Avatar, who "will be all-powerful and bear down everything before Him."[4]

After more than a quarter of a century of living in His Company, participating in His direct face-to-face Teaching Work with thousands of people, feeling the indescribable Transmission of Spirit-Force that Radiates from Him, and witnessing the limitless scope of His Divine Power to transform beings and conditions near and far, we, the devotees of Avatar Adi Da, freely profess our recognition that He is that All-Completing God-Man promised for the "dark" epoch—He is "the 'late-time' Avataric Revelation" of the Divine Person. Reading this book will enable you to make this supreme discovery for yourself.

The Work of the Promised God-Man in the World

Even the slightest gesture of Beloved Adi Da is for the Purpose of Liberating beings. This is His own Confession, the Truth of Which is witnessed daily by His devotees. His Work, as He Says, is at the "Source-Point", at the Place Where worlds arise out of the One Indivisible Light.

Inevitably, then, the Work of the Ruchira Avatar requires extraordinary Siddhis, or Divine Powers. Throughout His Lifetime, He has Miraculously healed many people. Remarkable weather phenomena frequently accompany His movements. And, time and again, global conflicts to which He Gives His Regard have been seen to resolve, inexplicably.

At the same time, His Work is not superficially "magical". Avatar Adi Da Samraj is not here to create utopia, or a paradise for egos. Rather, He is Working to counter the egoic, separative forces that create conflict, destruction, and suffering of all kinds. He is Working at the heart of all beings, Drawing them into Communion with Him, Awakening their Impulse to the Divine, to That Which Is Beyond the apparently separate self.

The Compassionate Work of the Ruchira Avatar, Adi Da Samraj, goes on simultaneously at every level—He may appear, on the ordinary level, to be Working with a particular human being in His immediate Company, but at the same time, He is Giving His Regard to events and conditions in the natural world, in the arena of global conflicts and politics, and in the domain of non-human beings, including the spirit-realms.

In the light of Avatar Adi Da's Revelation, all the great Realizers of the past are seen to be His forerunners, preparing for and converging toward the moment when the Divine could finally Appear Most Perfectly in bodily (human) Form. Beloved Adi Da Appears in an era when our very survival is threatened, not only by sophisticated weapons of war, but also by the destruction of human culture—and even of our total environment—through the heartless machine of scientific and political materialism. Miraculously, in this extreme time, Avatar Adi Da Samraj is here—here to allay the forces of destruction, here to Establish His Great Divine Way, the True World-Religion of Adidam. As He has Said Himself, it may take thousands of years for the significance of His Birth—the Descent of the Divine Person into cosmic space and time—to be fully appreciated. But His Revelation has now perfectly and irrevocably occurred.

The Divine Names of the Ruchira Avatar

There are several parts to the Divine Title and Name of Ruchira Avatar Adi Da Samraj, each of which expresses an aspect of our recognition of Him. "Ruchira" (meaning "Radiant", "Effulgent", or "Bright") is the Condition of All-Pervading Radiance, Joy, and Love-Blissful Divine Consciousness, Which He, even in His infancy, named "the 'Bright'". Avatar Adi Da Samraj is the unique Revelation of the "Bright"—and, because this is so, He is the Ruchira "Avatar", or the "Shining Divine 'Descent'", the Appearance of Real God in bodily (human) Form.

"Adi Da", the Principal Name of our Beloved Guru, is a sublime Mystery in itself. In 1979, He Assumed the Divine Name "Da", an ancient reference to Real God (first spontaneously Revealed to Him in 1970), a Name that means "the Divine Giver". In 1994, the Name "Adi" (meaning "First", or "Source") came to Him spontaneously as the complement to His Principal Name, "Da". Thus, to call upon the Ruchira Avatar via the Name "Adi Da" is to Invoke Him as the Divine Giver and Source-Person, the Primordial and Eternal Being of Grace.

Avatar Adi Da is also "Samraj", the "Universal Ruler", or "Supreme Lord"—not in any worldly or political sense, but as the Divine Master of all hearts and the Spiritual King of all who resort to Him. Thus, when we approach Avatar Adi Da Samraj, we are not at all approaching an ordinary man, or even a remarkable saint or yogi or sage. We are approaching Real God in Person.

The Divine Body of Real God

What does this really mean? When devotees of the supreme God-Man Adi Da come into His physical Company, and especially when they sit before Him in formal silent occasions, remarkable things occur. Some describe the feeling (and even the sight) of an Infinitely "Bright", Infinitely Expansive "Shape" filling the space, Radiating beyond it, and, at the same time, pressing in upon their own body with a tangible Touch of utter Bliss and Love. Some from time to time have had the sense of becoming the form of Avatar Adi Da—the feeling that He is literally "replacing" their own body, head to toe, with His Body.

Stories of this kind are not reports of Spiritual experiences in the usual internal sense. These experiences are not happening "within" you. They are are as tangible and objective as a physical embrace. They come to you from without. You do not—you could not—generate them yourself.

Such experiences Reveal that the apparent, physical Body of Adi Da Samraj is just the minutest part of the Grand Scale of His Being, the part that has "Emerged" into visibility. His bodily (human) Form is simply a means, a touch-stone, by Which He Draws you into the Mystery that He is altogether. He is Consciousness Itself, Inherently Love-Blissful, Self-Radiant Being Itself. He is, in His own Words, "the True and Spiritual Divine Person", Who makes Himself known most intimately and ecstatically through the Revelation of His Divine Body—the Infinitely Expansive, Radiantly "Bright" Form of Real God:

AVATAR ADI DA SAMRAJ: My Divine Form Is the "Bright", the Love-Bliss-Form That you can feel tangibly Touching you, Surrounding you, Moving in you, Making all kinds of changes. That Is My Divine Body. I can Manifest It anywhere, and Do, all the time. I Manifest My Self.

My True Body, My Eternal Body Is the "Bright" Itself, My Force of Person. This physical Body here Is My Murti,[5] My Agent. This physical Body is utterly Conformed to Me, My "Bright" Divine Body, but this physical Body is Itself made of the elements, and associated with subtle faculties, and all the rest.

This physical Body, as I Said, Is My Murti, My Agent. It is temporary. I am using It for the Purpose of My Self-Revelation and for Instructing the world, but, even when this physical Body is no longer animated, I will Be Bodily Present Forever.

My Divine Body will Exist Forever. Therefore, My devotees will be able to experience Me directly, Bodily—My "Bright" Body, My Very Person—Forever.

The principal form of contact with Me is through feeling and through this tangible but inexplicable Touch. It even has a form to it that may be sensed in a touch-like manner, subtly, not otherwise being perceived by any of the senses.

I call My own Divine Body "the 'Bright'". That does not mean you will necessarily see it as "Brightness", but you might see it in some light-form. But even if you are simply feeling Me, experiencing My Tangible Touch, you still know what I mean when I call My Divine Body "the 'Bright'", because It Is Full and Radiant, Love-Blissful, Infinitely Expansive. It has all the qualities of brightness. [August 11, 1995]

The "Bright"

Avatar Adi Da was <u>born</u> as the "Bright". His human Birth (in New York, on November 3, 1939) made no change in His Consciousness. The Radiance, the unlimited Love-Bliss of the "Bright" was the constant experience of His early infancy. He knew Himself to Be the very Source of the "Bright", the True and "Bright" Condition of everything.

At the same time, Avatar Adi Da was perfectly Aware of everything around Him. He saw that people were not Happy, that each person presumed himself or herself to be separate from Real God (or from Truth, or from Reality Itself), and was struggling to deal with that feeling of separation and all the suffering that follows from it. Avatar Adi Da Samraj found this remarkable—it was not His experience at all, because He was not identified with an ordinary body-mind.

For His first two years, Adi Da Samraj Enjoyed the undiminished Bliss of His Real Condition. Then, during His second year, something mysterious occurred. As He was crawling across the linoleum floor one day, His parents let loose a new puppy they were giving Him—and in the instant of seeing the puppy and seeing His parents, Avatar Adi Da's relationship to His Infinite Awareness suddenly changed. He made the spontaneous choice to be an "I", an apparently separate person relating to apparently separate others.

"Forgetting" the "Bright"

What had happened? Adi Da Samraj had relinquished the "Bright", out of a "painful loving", a sympathy for the suffering and ignorance of human beings. He was demonstrating the Great Impulse behind His Birth—the Impulse to make the "Bright" known to every one. In His own Words, His Purpose in His human body was to "Learn Man" so that He could enter into everything that mankind feels and suffers, in order "To Teach and To Bless and To Liberate Man". The only way that Avatar Adi Da could fulfill this Purpose was to intentionally "forget" the "Bright", to experience life from the ordinary human point of view—and then, in the midst of that limited condition, to find the Way to recover the "Bright".

This was Avatar Adi Da's early-life Ordeal, and it was a perilous, desperate affair, with no guarantees as to how it would turn out. To relinquish all awareness of His Divine State and adapt to the ordinary human condition was the most daring Gesture. It was the willing Embrace of an inconceivably difficult Ordeal, undertaken for the sake of all un-Illumined beings. None of it was necessary for His own Sake. His Life, then, as now, was Moved entirely by a Divine Impulse of Love and Compassion.

Avatar Adi Da had no "method" for recovering the "Bright". But He Embraced every aspect of human life, both great and ordinary, in order to Reveal the complete Truth of existence, the Truth that can set every one Free. Avatar Adi Da's recovery of the "Bright" was a most intense Ordeal that lasted for His first thirty years.

In the course of this Process, Adi Da Samraj always risked everything for the Truth. He could not bear to place any limitations on His quest to recover the "Bright". In this disposition, Avatar Adi Da not only thoroughly explored the realms of ordinary human experience, but He also passed through every possible kind of psychic and Spiritual Awakening—and with extraordinary speed. It was as if these Awakenings were already, in some sense, thoroughly familiar to Him.

However, Avatar Adi Da was not satisfied. He had the intuition of some "incredible Knowledge". He knew that the ultimate Truth had to be the Source-Condition of any of these experiences, any of these visions, any moment of revelation. The hidden Force of the "Bright" Itself was always Alive in Him, leading Him toward the perfect fulfillment of His quest.

Having been born into the twentieth-century West (with its denial of the esoteric dimension of religious and Spiritual life), Avatar Adi Da grew up with no knowledge of the Guru-devotee relationship. He discovered the Liberating Bond of Guru-Love just as spontaneously as He discovered everything else in the Process of His Divine Re-Awakening.

His first Teacher was an American—Swami Rudrananda (also known as "Rudi"). Rudi, who Taught in New York City, Guided Adi Da Samraj in the preliminary stages of His Spiritual growth, and, later, passed Adi Da on to his own Lineage of Gurus in India—Swami Muktananda and Swami Nityananda.

Avatar Adi Da's Gurus were extraordinary Realizers. They were Siddhas, Yogis alive with Spiritual Power. He submitted to their Instruction and their discipline with limitless devotion and heart-felt gratitude. But Avatar Adi Da

Swami Rudrananda

Swami Muktananda

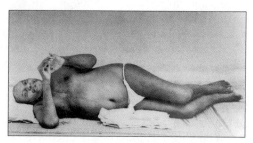

Swami Nityananda

did not do this for His own Sake. His Submission to His Gurus was part of His Submission to the human Ordeal altogether—in this case to the Spiritual Process as it had been traditionally experienced. He needed to discover everything about the esoteric anatomy and the Yogic Realizations potential in every human body-mind, so that He could Instruct and Guide His future devotees—and every one—in the transcending of _all_ experience, including the entire range of Spiritual experience.

All kinds of Spiritual Realizations are described in the traditions, and Adi Da Samraj passed through all of them—

visions, trances, mystical raptures, "Cosmic Consciousness", states of profound meditation and Transcendental "Knowledge". But in the closing phases of His Ordeal of Spiritual Realization, Avatar Adi Da's overwhelming Impulse to the Truth drove Him into territory unknown to His Gurus, unknown in the annals of Spiritual literature. His ultimate Divine Re-Awakening to the "Bright" occurred on the basis of a unique and all-encompassing insight, a "radical"[6] understanding that places mankind's entire history of Spiritual seeking and Realization in a new light—and leads beyond all of it.

"Radical" Understanding

When Adi Da Samraj Speaks of "'radical' understanding", or just "understanding", He is referring to a most profound and liberating insight—a direct awareness of the single root-cause behind all un-Happiness. He is pointing to something we are always doing, an activity that is actually holding back the flood-gates of Divine Bliss, Joy, Happiness, and Love. What is that Happiness-preventing activity exactly? What is it that we are doing that is keeping us from Realizing the "Bright" right now?

Avatar Adi Da found out.

Through the most rigorous observation of Himself in every possible circumstance—while talking, reading, dreaming, eating, at the movies, at a party, walking alone—this primal activity more and more stood out in His awareness. He saw that we are always contracting—recoiling from existence, physically, emotionally, mentally, psychically. This self-contraction, Adi Da Samraj came to see, is our constant, though largely unconscious, response to the uncontrollable, unknowable world in which we find ourselves. It is a fearful reaction to the fact that we know we are going to die. And its effects are devastating.

The self-contraction, Adi Da Samraj realized, is the source of fear, sorrow, anger, desire, guilt, competitive-

19

ness, shame, and all the mayhem of this world. Even ordinary pleasurable moments are governed by the same root-activity. It became undeniably obvious to Avatar Adi Da that everything we do is a form of search, an effort to be free of the self-inflicted pain of self-contraction. But this effort cannot succeed, because the search itself is a form of the self-contraction. Therefore, the effort of seeking for Release, for Freedom, cannot lead us to the Happiness we desire. Perfect Truth, or unqualified Happiness, Adi Da saw, only appears when the activity of self-contraction is "radically" understood, and, thereby, spontaneously released—revealing the Simplicity, the Joy of Being That Is Always Already the Case.

The awakening of "radical" understanding may sound simple—but do not be deceived. It is a most profound process. The self-contraction is programmed into the very cells of the body. Therefore, "radical" understanding can only awaken in ordinary human beings by the Grace of Avatar Adi Da Himself, and on the basis of the total practice of the Divine Way only He has Revealed and Given, the Way of Adidam.

During the years of His "Sadhana", or Spiritual practice, Adi Da Samraj awakened to "radical" self-understanding through the Force of His Very Being, the "Bright" Itself. And even after this fundamental intuition arose in Him, Avatar Adi Da could not instantaneously correct the fault—because He had submitted to all the limits of human existence. But Avatar Adi Da's unique understanding, once it was fundamentally established, accelerated the entire Process of His Divine Re-Awakening. It proved to be a kind of "muscle", an insight that gave Him the key to every experience, high and low.

As He moved closer to the great resolution of His early-life Ordeal, Adi Da Samraj observed the self-contraction in more and more subtle forms. He observed it even as the simplest awareness of separateness, the naked sense of "I" and "other" that is at the root of our perception of the world.

By now, it was obvious to Him that the self-contraction explained not only the ordinary dramas of life, but the entire "tour" of Spiritual experience as well. At last, it became obvious to Avatar Adi Da that all of mankind's searches for Real God (or for Truth, or for Reality Itself) were an immense effort of seeking that was totally unnecessary, based on a fundamental error—the lack of "radical" understanding. Then there was not anything left over, there was not anything left for Him to Realize, except the Truth Itself.

Re-Awakening to the "Bright"

Secluded in a corner of Hollywood is a small temple, established by the Vedanta Society of Southern California. This simple temple, standing in the shadow of a giant freeway, provided the setting for the culminating Event of Avatar Adi Da's Spiritual Ordeal. Adi Da Samraj discovered the temple in August 1970, and began to go there frequently for meditation. One day, September 10, He went and sat in the temple as usual:

As time passed, there was no Event of changes, no movement at all. There was not even any kind of inward deepening, no "inwardness" at all. There was no meditation. There was no need for meditation. There was not a single element or change that could be added to make my State Complete. I sat with my eyes open. I was not having an experience of any kind. Then, suddenly, I understood most perfectly.[7] I Realized that I had Realized. The "Thing" about the "Bright" became Obvious. I Am Complete. I Am the One Who Is Complete.

In That instant, I understood and Realized (inherently, and most perfectly) What and Who I Am. It was a tacit Realization, a direct Knowledge in Consciousness: It was Consciousness Itself, without the addition of a Communication from any "Other" Source. There Is no "Other" Source. I simply sat there and Knew What and Who I Am. I was Being What I Am, Who I Am. I Am Being What I Am, Who I Am. I Am Reality, the Divine Self, the Nature, Substance, Support, and Source of all things and all beings. I Am the One Being, called "God" (the Source and Substance and Support and Self of all), the "One Mind" (the Consciousness and Energy in and As Which all appears), "Siva-Shakti"[8] (the Self-Existing and Self-Radiant Reality Itself), "Brahman"[9] (the Only Reality, Itself), the "One Atman"[10] (That Is not ego, but Only "Brahman", the Only Reality, Itself), the "Nirvanic Ground"[11] (the egoless and conditionless Reality and Truth, Prior to all dualities, but excluding none). I Am the One and Only and necessarily Divine Self, Nature, Condition, Substance, Support, Source, and Ground of all. I Am the "Bright". [The Knee Of Listening]

This unspeakable Moment was the Divine Re-Awakening of the Ruchira Avatar, Adi Da Samraj. He had permanently and Most Perfectly Re-Awakened to the "Bright". His Realization was not dependent on meditative states, or on any manipulation of experience. It transcended even the slightest sense of identity as a separate self. It was and is the Realization that There Is Only Real God and that all apparent events are simply the passing forms, or modifications, of Real God, arising and dissolving in an endless Play that is Bliss and Love beyond comprehension.

The very Divine Person had become Perfectly Conscious and Present through an ordinary human vehicle. In all the eons of cosmic time, this Great Event was unprecedented. Avatar Adi Da's utter transcending of the limits of human existence in all its dimensions—physical, mental, emotional, psychic, Spiritual—was total, Perfect, and Complete. Avatar Adi Da Samraj had Realized Absolute Identity with the Divine, the One He Was, and Is, from the beginning. But His Divine Re-Awakening signified far more than this. It was also the Revelation that all apparently separate beings Are also only That Very One, and can—through right, true, full, and fully devotional recognition of Avatar Adi Da, and right, true, full, and fully devotional response to Him—Realize this same Truth. The Condition of the "Bright", the Real-God-Light of Avatar Adi Da's birth and infancy, was now Fully Established—not only in Him, but as the native Truth and the potential Realization of all beings in all worlds.

Through the Power of Avatar Adi Da's Re-Awakening to the "Bright", something has changed at the very heart of existence. The Ruchira Avatar, Adi Da Samraj, has Done What only the Divine could Do. He has, so to speak, "cracked the cosmic code", broken through the force of illusion that has always kept born beings bound to the realms of change and suffering and death.

The Teaching Work Begins

After His Divine Re-Awakening in 1970, Adi Da Samraj was consumed with an almost intolerable Urgency to lead others through the great Process of Liberation that He Himself had Discovered. In 1971 He wrote in His journals that He felt like Ramakrishna pacing the temple roof in Dakshineswar wailing for his devotees, those he knew must come.[12] He literally felt His future devotees crowding in upon Him in vision. He was already "Meditating" them, and Drawing them into His physical Company. And soon His Teaching Work did begin, in the back rooms of a small bookstore in Hollywood, California.

Los Angeles, 1972

The Teaching Work of Adi Da Samraj marked a new level of His Submission to the human condition. He gave Himself up completely once more, this time to suffer the process with all those who came to Him, determined to Give them the "real thing", the living Process of God-Realization rather than merely a "talking" school conversation about Ultimate Truth.

Everything that we do, everything that we desire and fear, everything that human beings have ever experienced or puzzled about was explored by Adi Da face to face with His devotees, in minute and exhaustive detail. There is an entire archive of His conversations with devotees— on Spiritual experience, on sacred culture and the arts, on diet, exercise and breathing, sex and intimacy, childrearing, science and the psycho-physical nature of the world, death and reincarnation, and on and on.

During that extraordinary exploration, Avatar Adi Da Revealed the right life-practice in all the areas of functional existence—how to eat, how to breathe, how to exercise, how to make love, how to relate to every kind of circumstance such that heart-Communion with Him is maintained undiminished in the midst of ordinary life and the body-mind is made into a Yogic vehicle able to receive and conduct His Spirit-Force.

It was through this profound "consideration" of the needs and questions of every one who came to Him that Adi Da Samraj established the religion of Adidam, or the Way of the Heart, and created the sacred culture of His devotees that exists today around the world.

The Divine "Crazy" Man

From the early days of His Teaching Work, Adi Da Samraj would not merely speak to His devotees, or engage in Dharmic dialogue. He would always create incident as well—a meal, a party, a pool game, a fishing trip, a movie, a swimming occasion, some interactive setting (which might continue all day and night) in which He could observe people relating directly to Him and to each other. No one ever knew what would occur, what the lessons would be, or where the occasion would go. But you could predict that the Divine Avatar would make His famous Remarks (often outrageously funny) that would instantly reflect to you your characteristic fears, your self-protectiveness, your seeking for attention, and would bring to light feelings and reactions that you did not know were in you until that moment.

Adi Da Samraj is the Divine "Crazy" Man, or Avadhoot,[13] an absolutely Free Being, untrammeled by social or religious conventions. The true Avadhoot is "dangerous" to the ego. He uses His Freedom to Awaken others, always doing everything possible to show people where and how they are bound, un-Happy, stuck, and un-Illumined. He has used every means to give the revelation of "Narcissus"— the "I" that is always turning away from others, from life, from Real God—to His devotees.

Human beings refuse the Divine, refuse their own greatest Help. The egoic self wants to be left alone to be the ruler in its own castle. This has been the most sobering

with devotees in California, 1974

lesson for all of Adi Da's devotees—thrilled, delighted to be in the Company of the Living One, and yet, at some level, resisting Him, not wanting to surrender the separate and separative ego-"I".

And so Adi Da will often Speak fiercely, He will Say or Do conventionally "forbidden" things, or ask for things to be accomplished which feel like impossible feats from the ordinary point of view. He is constantly taking you beyond your presumed limitations on energy, beyond your fears, beyond the place where you want to resist or refuse, requiring you to come to a deeper level of surrender to Him and a higher level of functioning in every aspect of life.

In times past, people were cautioned never to approach an Avadhoot casually, because of the purifying Spiritual energies (having their own laws and consequences) that are activated in a relationship to such a one. However, it was also understood that a mature practitioner making a right and humble approach to the fire of the Avadhoot could burn off much karma and accelerate the Spiritual Process. In the Company of Avatar Adi Da Samraj, the same Process, raised to the Divine Level, takes place. He is the Fire of Very God, purifying all, and so, if you stay with the "heat" of the Process, and do not withdraw from Him, your growth can be dramatic. Countless beings may be affected by the surrender of even one devotee, because Avatar Adi Da Works with every one through those who are devotionally linked to Him. Avatar Adi Da is always pointing to the alternative to "Narcissus": The simple act of turning to Him, receiving His Help, His complete Acceptance and Love. In the instant of His Addressing a devotee—Humorously, Critically, Sweetly, Forcefully—He is making an opening in that individual (and in the Cosmos itself) to receive more of His Grace. That Grace is a Spiritual Transmission of His Divine Love-Bliss, a Blessing beyond price, Which Pervades the body-mind and, ultimately, Moves the devotee beyond the body-mind altogether.

The Supreme Tantric Master

The Way of Adidam, however, is not about denying the body or escaping from the world. Adi Da Himself has assumed a body, assumed it down to the toes, and there is no trace in Him of puritanism or suppressiveness. He is the Divine Tantric Master.

Tantra is popularly thought to be just about sex, but the true tradition of Tantra is the Spiritual discipline of turning all human functions (including sex) into Divine Communion, rather than simply avoiding, or indulging in, or being deluded or degraded by any dimension of life.

Avatar Adi Da, from the beginning, Called His devotees to freely examine all taboos. He Addressed their unconscious relationship to food, their anxiety and taboos relative to bodily functions, their obssessive sexual impulses, and their entire emotional life with profound force of "consideration", in order to Move them into the depth position of feeling and of sensitivity to the Spiritual Reality. He Addressed every tendency to shut down the life-force and suppress the heart. And He did all of that for the sake of creating the open, radiant equanimity in the body-mind that is the necessary foundation for Divine Enlightenment.

Avatar Adi Da Samraj is a Ruchira Tantric <u>Sannyasin</u>,[14] a Free Renunciate. Many traditional renunciates cut themselves off from the world in order to concentrate on the Spiritual Reality, but the Ruchira Tantric Sannyasin Realizes the Spiritual Reality in the midst of life. Avatar Adi Da is the <u>Supreme</u> Ruchira Tantric Sannyasin. He does not cut off anything, does not avoid anything, but simply Shines through every situation. He is neither "for" nor "against"— neither attached to nor opposed to—any ordinary (or extraordinary) form of experience. He Transcends <u>all</u> experience, while fully Responding to whatever is brought to Him—more Compassionately, more creatively than any mere human being could possibly do.

The Divine "Emergence"

Throughout His Teaching Years, Avatar Adi Da Samraj was laying the foundation for an infinitely greater, eternal Process whereby His Work would become truly effective and Liberating for every one. Early on the morning of January 11, 1986, an Event occurred at Adidam Samrajashram, Fiji, Which Initiated that eternal Process.

The moment, on the surface, was extremely disturbing and inauspicious. Avatar Adi Da Samraj had come to the point of utter, complete frustration with His devotees. We simply had not understood, most fundamentally, His "radical" Message about the fruitlessness of seeking and the inherent suffering of egoic life. And so, as much as we loved Him, followed Him, and served Him with good-hearted enthusiasm, there was no profound heart-turning to Him as the Living Form of Real God, the Only Help in the midst of ego-bondage.

Avatar Adi Da was on the phone to some of His devotees telling them that He felt His Life ebbing away because there was no response in them strong enough to hold Him in the body. As He spoke, one devotee went running to His

House and held Him as he continued to speak. But then Avatar Adi Da fell to the floor and dropped the telephone. The other devotees came running immediately and found the Divine Avatar slumped on the floor beside His bed and starting to show all the signs of physical death. While the doctors bent over Him looking for the faintest signs of life, devotees wept and prayed and called to Him not to leave.

Gradually Avatar Adi Da reassociated with the body. And then, suddenly, He sat up and pressed everyone back with a sweep of His arm and a profound cry of anguish. He was weeping for the "four billion", He said—all the human beings alive on this planet—weeping that He could not "Kiss" each one personally.

Weeks later, Avatar Adi Da Spoke about the meaning of that Great Event.

AVATAR ADI DA SAMRAJ: In this Great Event, I was drawn further into the body with a very human impulse, a love-impulse. Becoming aware of My profound relationship with all My devotees, I resumed My bodily human state. Even though I have existed as a man during this Lifetime, obviously—I became profoundly Incarnate—I now assumed an impulse toward human existence more profound than I had assumed before, without any reluctance relative to sorrow and death.

On so many occasions, I have Told you that I wish I could Kiss every human being on the lips, Embrace each one, and Enliven each one from the heart. In this body, I will never have the opportunity. I am frustrated in that Impulse. But in that Motion of sympathetic Incarnation, that acceptance of the body and its sorrow and its death, I Realized a Kiss, a way to fulfill the Impulse.

To Me, this is a Grand Victory! I do not know how to Communicate to you the significance of it. It seems that through that will-less, effortless integration with suffering, something about My Work is more profoundly accomplished, something about it has become more auspicious,

After the Divine "Emergence", 1986

than it ever was. I have not dissociated from My Realiza-
tion or My Ultimate State. Rather, I have accomplished your
state completely, even more profoundly than you are sensi-
tive to it. Perhaps you have seen it in My face. I have
become this body, utterly. My mood is different. My face is
sad, although not without Illumination. I have become the
body. Now I am the "Murti", the Icon, and It is Full of the
Divine Presence. [January 27, 1986]

The Great Event of January 11, as Avatar Adi Da later
explained, was, in fact, the most profound Yogic Swoon,
and not a near-death moment in the conventional sense. In
that Swoon, the Divine Avatar spontaneously relinquished
His Teaching Work and His pattern of identification with
others in order to Awaken them. In other words, He utterly

surrendered His body-mind—the conditional Vehicle of His Incarnation—into His own Very Being, the Grace and Power and "Brightness" of Da, the Eternal Divine Person.

When devotees were Graced to behold Avatar Adi Da in the weeks and months following this momentous Event, they were struck to the depths by His "Brightness". He was Transparent to His Divinity as never before, and He was Awakening in people, even many who had never seen Him before, an undeniable Knowledge, the most direct, and ecstatic and heart-breaking recognition of Him As the Very Divine Person.

January 11, 1986 was the Initiation of the full Divine "Emergence" of Avatar Adi Da Samraj, the culmination of the Process of His Birth, His "Sadhana Years", His Divine Re-Awakening, and His subsequent Work to Teach and Awaken suffering beings. It was the beginning of the era of His universal Blessing Work.

The End of the Twenty-Five Year Revelation

Even after the Great Event in 1986 that initiated His Divine "Emergence", Avatar Adi Da continued to Work to ensure that His Revelation of the Way of Adidam, the unique Divine Way of Realizing Real God, was fully and firmly founded in the world. It was not until March 1997 that Avatar Adi Da Samraj Declared that all the foundation Work of His Incarnation had been completely and finally Done.

The inexpressible Divine Sacrifice of Avatar Adi Da Samraj is Full. Everything, absolutely everything, necessary for the total Great Process of Divine Enlightenment has been Said and Done by Him. His Divine Wisdom-Teaching is preserved for all time in His twenty-three "Source-Texts". And His Divine Way, the Way of Adidam, is fully established. All in all, this monumental Work has taken Avatar Adi Da a quarter of a century—twenty-five years of unrelenting Struggle to make His Avataric Incarnation real in the hearts and body-minds of His devotees.

AVATAR ADI DA SAMRAJ: I have "Meditated" every one, every thing—all that I have had to assume, take on, submit to, combine with, identify with, and so forth, all that I have had to struggle with, endure—everything altogether of the last twenty-five years. During all these years in this bodily Manifestation here, I have Submitted to everything associated with the gross personality (in other words, the gross aspect of My Appearance here), everything associated with the Deeper-Personality dimension—all aspects of the Vehicle. I did not exclude anything from My "Meditation", My "Consideration".

I have over and over again Communicated to every one, all those years, that the Way of Adidam is this relationship to Me. The Way of Adidam is the life you live when you rightly, truly, fully, and fully devotionally recognize Me and rightly, truly, fully, and fully devotionally respond to Me. [May 20, 1997]

The rest of the bodily human Lifetime of Avatar Adi Da Samraj is simply for the sake of His Blessing of all, and also for the sake of His esoteric Work with formal renunciate devotees.[15] Avatar Adi Da is fiercely Intent upon this Work with His renunciates. He must have such devotees, completely given over to Him, whom He can Awaken to His Divinely Enlightened Condition in this lifetime. This must be so if He is to have Means for His Blessing and Awakening Grace to be passed into the future with full authenticity.

Avatar Adi Da Samraj Resides at His Principal Hermitage—Naitauba Island, or Adidam Samrajashram, in Fiji—except when He is moved to travel for the sake of His Blessing Work. But, even when He is travelling, Adi Da does not function as a public Teacher, and never has. His Spiritual Blessing goes to every one and all, but, generally speaking, only those who have taken formal vows of devotion to Him come into His personal Company. This has always been the pattern of His Work, because the Process of Divine Awakening in His Company is the most serious

32

Spiritual matter, requiring full devotional recognition of Avatar Adi Da as the Divine Person Incarnate and deeply heart-felt obedience to His Instructions.

AVATAR ADI DA SAMRAJ: The true heart-relationship must be established with Me. You come to Me, but then you get to My Chair and you do not have anything. Everybody is the same. In other words, it is not a social matter, and it does not require conversations in which I need to repeat My Teaching to You. I have Said what needed to be said. Study that "consideration".

My own Work goes on. People come and sit in My House. There are places provided for an even flow of people to come. That is what I am here to Do. I am just going to Do My Work. I am here to see people gather around Me to do this, very intensively, day after day. [April 11, 1997]

The Way of Adidam

The immense struggle and Sacrifice that the Divine Avatar had to endure in order to make His Revelation of the Divine Way of Adidam was the result of the enormous difficulty that human beings—especially in this ego-glorifying "late-time"—have with the Process of truly ego-transcending religion. People prefer not to confront the real Process of ego-transcendence. They prefer forms of religion based on a system of beliefs and a code of moral and social behavior. But this kind of ordinary religion, as Avatar Adi Da has always pointed out, does not go to the core, to the root-suffering of human beings. This is because ordinary religion, rather than going beyond the ego-principle, is actually based on it: the ego-self stands at the center, and the Divine is sought and appealed to as the great Power that is going to save and satisfy the individual self. Avatar Adi Da Describes such religion as "client-centered".

In contrast to conventional religion, there is the Process that Avatar Adi Da calls true religion, religion that is centered in the Divine in response to a true Spiritual Master, who has, to at least some significant degree, Realized Real God (as opposed to merely offering teachings about God). Thus, true religion does not revolve around the individual's desires for any kind of "spiritual" consolations or experience—it is self-transcending, rather than self-serving. True religion based on self-surrendering Guru-devotion certainly has existed for thousands of years, but the ecstatic news of this book is that now the Divine Person, Real God, is directly Present, Functioning as Guru, Alive in bodily (human) Form to receive the surrender and the worship of those who recognize and respond to Him. Therefore, the Ruchira-Guru, Adi Da, is the Way of Adidam.

The word "Adidam" is derived from the Name of Ruchira Avatar Adi Da, because it is the religion founded on devotional recognition of Him and Spiritual resort to Him. This Spiritual resort to Beloved Adi Da is a moment to moment practice of surrendering every aspect of the being—mind, emotion, breath, and body—to Him. Such whole-bodily surrender to the Living One opens the heart to Joy. Thus, in the Way of Adidam there is no struggle to overcome egoity or to achieve Oneness with God. Real God is already Revealed and may be "Located" via heart-Communion with Adi Da Samraj in every moment. In His Spiritual Company, therefore, there is not anything to seek, as He Describes here. This is the "radical" nature of the Way of Adidam, compared with traditional religion, which is essentially based on the search for God.

AVATAR ADI DA SAMRAJ: The traditional religious and Spiritual Ways have always been based on seeking, or the exercise of egoity itself. All of the traditional Ways have that characteristic.

The basic point of view of the seeker is "I am not yet Realized", "I am not yet experienced", "I am not yet here". From this point of view, the seeker must do something, or go somewhere, or achieve an alternative position in order to enter into Divine Communion, or Divine Realization.

The act of egoity generates the experiential presumption that gross psycho-physical embodiment is inherently dissociated from the Divine Condition. Therefore, until My Avataric-Incarnation-Appearance here, it has been universally presumed that a search is required in order to attain the Divine Condition, or the Divine Domain. That very point of view is *the ego speaking, the ego proposing, the self-contraction making the "Way". Such is not the characteristic of Adidam.*

The Way of Adidam is the Way That is always *Prior to and Beyond all seeking. In order for the Way of Adidam to be Generated, it was necessary for Me to be Incarnated, and Transmitted in place, in this place, in the extremity— in the place where the Divine is otherwise not proposed, or is only sought. This was necessary, in order to Demonstrate that I Am That One Who Is Always Already The Case, and in order to Communicate the Way of non-seeking, or the Way of transcending egoity in* this *circumstance of arising (or in any circumstance of arising).*

The "problem" is not that the Divine is "Elsewhere". The "problem" is that you *are the* self-contraction*. This understanding, Given by My Grace, makes it possible to Realize the Divine Self-Condition Most Perfectly,* As Is, *no matter what is arising. But Such Most Perfect Realization is not merely Realization of the Divine as an abstract (or merely philosophically proposed) "Reality". Most Perfect Realization (or Most Perfect "Knowledge") of the Divine is the Divine "Known" by Means of My Revelation, "Known"* As *My Revelation.*

I *Came to* you*. Therefore, the Way of Adidam is based on your* receiving *Me, not on your* seeking *for Me.*

Thus, That Which is proposed by seekers as the goal *(or the achievement at the end) is the* beginning *(or the very Gift) of the Way for My devotees.* ["I Am The Avatar Of One", from Part Two of *He-and-She Is Me*]

All religious seeking—for the Vision of God, or for Oneness with Reality via the samadhis, satoris, and mystical experiences described in the traditions—falls away when the heart falls in love with Adi Da Samraj. He is Perfect Satisfaction, because He is Real God, the Very Source and Giver of true religion.

Like all true religious and Spiritual practice, the sadhana of Adidam is a Process of Liberation—Liberation from the illusion of identification with the separate and dying body-mind and Realization, to one or another degree, of the eternal Non-separate Condition of Being Itself. But the Way of Adidam offers more than the Realizations described in the religious and Spiritual traditions. It is the Process of Divine Liberation, Divine Self-Realization, Divine Enlightenment, uniquely Revealed by Avatar Adi Da.

Divine Enlightenment is the Realization of "No-Difference" between Consciousness Itself and the world (or what arises to Consciousness). Divine Enlightenment, in the Glorious Words of Adi Da, is Realization of "Indivisible Oneness with Real God". Thus, to be Divinely Enlightened is to Divinely Recognize all phenomena and all experience, high or low, as mere and unnecessary modifications of the One Conscious Radiance of Real God.

The entire Spiritual Process culminating in Divine Enlightenment has been exactly "mapped" by Avatar Adi Da, Who Describes It in terms of seven stages of life. In the total (or full and complete) practice of the Way of Adidam, the seven stages of life are, from first to last, a Process in Consciousness, Revealing (ultimately) that you Are Consciousness, and not merely the body-mind.

The first three (or foundation) stages of life constitute the ordinary course of human adaptation—bodily, emotional, and mental growth. The fourth and fifth (or advanced) stages of life are characterized by the Awakening to Spirit, or the Spiritualizing of the body-mind.

In the sixth and seventh (or ultimate) stages of life, Consciousness Itself is directly Realized, beyond identification with the body-mind. In the sixth stage of life, the Real-izer Identifies with Consciousness (in profound states of meditation) by excluding all awareness of phenomena. Avatar Adi Da has Revealed that this was the highest form of Realization known in the religious and Spiritual tradi-tions previous to His Appearance. But this Realization is incomplete. Even the necessity to turn away from the world in order to fully Enjoy Consciousness represents a contraction, a refusal of Reality in its totality. The seventh stage of life, or the Realization of "Open Eyes", transcends this last limit. No exclusion is necessary, because the world is Realized to be a mere modification of Consciousness, not separate (or "different") from Consciousness at all.

In His vast commentaries on the Great Tradition of religion and Spirituality,[16] Avatar Adi Da has Revealed that all traditional forms of Enlightenment—degrees of Com-munion with the Divine, union with Divine, or Oneness with Transcendental Consciousness—represent the partial Realizations of either the fourth stage of life, the fifth stage of life, or the sixth stage of life.[17] The seventh stage of life is the Realization of the "Bright" Itself, the Perfectly Love-Bliss-Full Divine Self-Condition of the Very Divine Person. Avatar Adi Da Samraj Is the Ruchira Avatar, the Unique Descent of the "Bright" into the Cosmic domain, and, thus, He Is the First, the Last, and the Only Adept-Realizer of the seventh stage of life, Present to Awaken the Supreme Realization of the "Bright" in His devotees. Avatar Adi Da Speaks here of how He has brought the seventh stage Revelation into the conditional worlds for the first time:

In and by Means of My Avataric Incarnation here (and every "where" in the Cosmic domain), I Am Self-Manifested (and, temporarily, or conditionally, Manifested) As the Ruchira Avatar, Adi Da Samraj, the first, the last, and the only Adept-Realizer of the seventh stage of life.

Until My Avataric Incarnation As the Ruchira Avatar, Adi Da Samraj, there has never been a seventh stage Adept-

Realizer here (or any "where" in the Cosmic domain).

I Am the Ruchira Avatar, Adi Da Samraj, the Realizer, the Revealer, and the Revelation of the seventh stage of life.

And I Am Da, That Which Is Realized in the seventh stage of life.

I Am the One to Be Realized by all and All.

I Am—Always Already The Case, now, and forever hereafter. . . .

The seventh stage Realization Is the Most Perfect Realization of Reality, Truth, or Real God (the One and Only Reality and Truth—the Only and Non-Separate One, Who Is, and That Is, Always Already The Case).

Only That One Can Make (and, now, Has Made, and Will, here, and every "where", forever hereafter, Make) This Divine Revelation and Accomplish This Divine Work.

Aham Da Asmi. Beloved, I Am That One—and (you must and will Realize, Most Perfectly) I Am always "Living" you, and I Am always "Breathing" you, and I Am always "Being" you, and I Always Already Am you (Beyond your ego-"I" of suffered, and always merely self-made, "difference"). ["I Am The Perfectly Subjective Divine Person, Self-Manifested As The Ruchira Avatar, Who Is The First, The Last, and The Only Adept-Realizer, Adept-Revealer, and Adept-Revelation of The Seventh Stage of Life", *The Seven Stages Of Life*]

Through the Grace of the Ruchira Avatar, Adi Da Samraj, the seventh stage of life, or Divine Enlightenment, is now possible for human beings for the first time. "Mankind", as Avatar Adi Da Says, "does not know the Way to the Divine Domain"—the ego does not know. Only the Divine Person Knows. Only the Divine Person, Incarnate as Guru, can Show you the Way to the Divine Domain.

The practice of Adidam is initiated by formally taking a sacred vow of devotion[18] to Avatar Adi Da Samraj. The vow is eternal because He is Eternal. The "Bond" with Him, once established, can never come to an end. It is unaffected by numberless deaths and rebirths, in this world or in any world.

Through this profound relationship with Avatar Adi Da, you are, over time, loosed from bondage to every kind of self-concern and your point of view relative to existence changes entirely. You become sensitive to Reality as a dynamic Spiritual Process, and you realize that the physical level of appearances is merely the outer shell of what exists.

In the ultimate stages of the practice of Adidam, when the body-mind is perfectly surrendered, the sense that Avatar Adi Da is an "Other" (to Whom you are relating) loses its hold on you. In that extraordinary transition, the movement to Communion with the Ruchira Avatar gives way to spontaneous and Most Blissful heart-Identification with Him. He Reveals Himself as Consciousness Only, Consciousness <u>Itself</u>, the Very Condition of all, including your own apparent body-mind.

Avatar Adi Da Samraj is directly Generating the Divine Process of Most Perfect Liberation in all His devotees who have vowed to embrace the total practice of the Way of Adidam.[19] The Process unfolds by His Grace, according to the depth of surrender and response in His devotee. The most extraordinary living testimonies to the Greatness and Truth of the Way of Adidam are Ruchira Adidama Sukha Dham Naitauba and Ruchira Adidama Jangama Hriddaya Naitauba, the two members of the Adidama Quandra Mandala of the Ruchira Avatar.[20] These remarkable women devotees have totally consecrated themselves to Avatar Adi Da, and live always in His Sphere, in a relationship of unique intimacy and service. By their profound love of, and most exemplary surrender to, their Divine Heart-Master, they have become combined with Him at a unique depth. They manifest the Yogic signs of deep and constant Immersion in His Divine Being, both in meditation and daily life. Ruchira Adidama Sukha Dham and Ruchira Adidama Jangama Hriddaya are also members of the Ruchira Sannyasin Order of the Tantric Renunciates of Adidam (the senior cultural authority within

**Avatar Adi Da Samraj with Ruchira Adidama Sukha Dham (left)
and Ruchira Adidama Jangama Hriddaya (right)**

the formal gathering of Avatar Adi Da's devotees), practicing in the context of the ultimate stages (or the "Perfect Practice") of the total Way of Adidam.

After more than twenty years of intense testing by their Beloved Guru, the Adidama Quandra Mandala have demonstrated themselves to be singular devotees, the first representatives of humankind to truly recognize Him As He Is. Through their profound recognition of Him, Avatar Adi Da has been able to lead the Adidama Quandra Mandala to the threshold of Divine Enlightenment. And, even now, day by day, He continues to Work with them to make their Realization of Him Most Perfect. The profound and ecstatic relationship that the Adidama Quandra Mandala live with Avatar Adi Da hour to hour can be felt in these letters of devotional confession to Him:

RUCHIRA ADIDAMA SUKHA DHAM: Bhagavan Love-Ananda,[21] Supreme and Divine Person, Real-God-Body of Love, I rest in Your Constant and Perfect Love-Embrace with no need but to forever worship you. Suddenly in love, Mastered at heart, always with my head at Your Supreme and Holy Feet, I am beholding and recognizing Your Divine

Body and "Bright" Divine Person. My Beloved, You so "Brightly" Descend and utterly Convert this heart, mind, body, and breath, from separate self to the "Bhava"[22] of Your Love-Bliss-Happiness.

Supreme Lord Ruchira, in the profound depths of Ruchira Sannyas (since my Initiation into formal Ruchira Sannyas on December 18, 1994), the abandonment of the former personality, the relinquishment of ego-bondage to the world, and the profound purification and release brought about by my now almost twenty-four years of love and worship of You has culminated in a great comprehensive force in my one-pointed devotion to You and a great certainty in the Inherent Sufficiency of Realization Itself. The essence, or depth, of my practice is to always remain freely submitted and centralized in You, the Feeling of Being, the Condition Prior to all bondage, all modification, and all illusion.

My Beloved Lord Ruchira, You have Moved this heart-feeling and awareness to renounce all "bonding" with conditionally manifested others, conditionally manifested worlds, and conditionally manifested self, to enter into the depths of this "in-love" and utter devotion to You. I renounce all in order to Realize You and to exist eternally in Your House. Finding You has led to the revelation of a deep urge to abandon all superficiality and to simply luxuriate in Your Divine Body and Person. All separation is shattered in Your Divine Love-Bliss-"Bhava". Your Divine and Supreme Body Surrounds and Pervades all. Your Infusion is Utter. I feel You everywhere.

I am Drawn by Grace of Your Spiritual (and Always Blessing) Presence into profound meditative Contemplation of Your Very (and Inherently Perfect) State. Sometimes, when I am entering into these deep states of meditation, I remain vaguely aware of the body, and particularly of the breath and the heartbeat. I feel the heart and lungs slow down and become very loud-sounding. Then I am sometimes aware of my breath and heartbeat ceasing temporarily, or being suspended in a state of Yogic sublimity, and I quickly lose bodily consciousness. Then there is no body, no mind, no perceptual awareness, and no conceptual awareness. There is only abiding in Contemplation of You in Your Domain of Consciousness Itself. I feel You literally Are me, and, when I resume association with the body and begin once again to hear my breath and heartbeat, I feel the remarkable Power of Your Great Samadhi. I feel no necessity for anything, and I feel Your Capability to Bless and Change and Meditate all, in Your Place. I can feel how this entrance into objectless worship of You As Consciousness Itself (allowing this Abiding to deepen ever so profoundly, by utter submission of separate self to You) establishes me in a different relationship to everything that arises.

My Beloved Bhagavan, Love-Ananda, I have Found You. Now I can behold You and live in this constant Embrace. This is my Joy and Happiness and the Yoga of ego-renunciation I engage. [October 11, 1997]

RUCHIRA ADIDAMA JANGAMA HRIDDAYA: My Dearly Beloved Adi Da Samraj, There are truly no words that can come close to describing the Miracle of all the Gifts that You Have Given to me. I lay myself at Your Sacred Feet in eternal gratitude and devotion. I love You, My Beloved Ishta-Guru,[23] with all my heart and with every cell of this body-mind, which is Yours. I make this confession of these Gifts with ecstasy and in praise of Your All-Accomplishing Work.

My Beloved, I know heart-deep that You Are Real God, the Divine Person Incarnate, the One That I and all beings have always prayed and waited for. I know that Your Divine

Siddhis are Complete, that You Are the Fulfillment of the Miraculous Sacred Process of Divine Descent, through Which Real God completely takes on the form of Man.

Beloved, You have enabled me to stably Stand as the Witness[24] in relation to all arisings in this body-mind and circumstantially. Particularly over the last year, this practice has deepened, and the steadiness of the depth-Realization in meditation has been strongly carrying into life, as You Admonished me that it must. I have felt You undoing the tendency to hold on to the Position of Consciousness as a Reality separate from Your Radiance (or Light), and I experience that error as a clear form of seeking (or un-Truth).

Through Your Skillful Means, You have Immersed me in Your Light and Love-Bliss and have required me to be actively engaged in transforming my life in surrender to You. In this way, You have brought me more and more to see and feel and Know You as the Conscious Being and Blissful Radiance Who Lives and Is all. I feel You all the time, Beloved, both in life and meditation, as "Atma-Murti", the Conscious Source-Condition of All and all. I Contemplate You as the Great Still-Point (or Well) of Being Itself, Consciousness Itself, Prior to all forms and thoughts and feelings and doings.

In that Well of Your Free Being, "I" become lost in a Swoon (or Samadhi) of no-attention to forms or thoughts or states or even the sense of "difference". This Samadhi is such a profound Gift of Your Hridaya-Shaktipat, My Beloved, that no words can even describe my gratitude. After attention begins to become reassociated with the body-mind, I notice that the heart and head and entire body-mind feel Flooded by Your Blissful, Radiant Love, and literally Infused with a different, freer perception of reality, Instilled with Your Conscious Being. I bow to You, My Divine Lord, for this Gift. I also intuit the limit of this Samadhi and how I am still bound by the delusion of Consciousness separated from form, not Divinely Recognizing all arising in and as only Consciousness-Radiance, Your Form Absolute. My Beloved, I pray with all of my heart that You Grant me this Realization by Your Grace. My heart longs for the Divine Realization of Perfect Inherence in You and Non-separation from You.

You Shine "Brighter" and "Brighter" before me, Beloved, and I prostrate at Your Feet in service and devotion to You. [October 11, 1997]

Inherent in these profound confessions is the certainty that there is no lasting happiness to be found in this world or in any world. The only real Happiness, the Happiness that infinitely exceeds all human dreams of Happiness, is the All-Outshining Bliss and Love of Heart-Realization of the Supreme Giver, Adi Da Samraj.

AVATAR ADI DA SAMRAJ: Absolutely NOTHING conditional is satisfactory. Everything conditional disappears—everything. This fact should move the heart to cling to Me, to resort to Me, to take refuge in Me. This is why people become devotees of Mine. This is the reason for the religious life. The unsatisfactoriness of conditional existence requires resort to the Divine Source, and the Realization of the Divine Source-Condition. [August 9, 1997]

A "Bright" New Age of Real-God-Man

Avatar Adi Da knew from His childhood that He had Come to "save the world". He even confessed as much to a relative who questioned him one day about what He wanted to do when He grew up.[25] But He did not mean this in any conventionally religious, or politically idealistic, sense. He has never taught a consoling belief system that promises "heaven" after death or a utopian existence on this earth. No, He has Come to set in motion a universal heart-conversion, a conversion from the self-destructive and other-destructive ego-life of separativeness to a life of "unqualified relatedness", or boundless all-embracing love. And He has always known that the only way to generate such great and even global change in the human disposition is to create a "seed", a sacred gathering of people who <u>are</u> living this way—living cooperatively from the non-egoic, or Real-God-Realizing, point of view.

Avatar Adi Da is constantly Working to establish such a gathering—a gathering of His true devotees who will incarnate, in every dimension of human life, the "Bright" Revelation He is Bringing to the world, and who will thereby make it possible for Him to Transform mankind, averting the otherwise dreadful destiny of possible global destruction.

Avatar Adi Da Samraj Speaks of His profound Vision of the future Work and Sign of His true devotees in His Essay "I Have Come To Found A 'Bright' New Age Of Real-God-Man". This Essay, the ending of which is quoted below, stands as one of His most extraordinary and significant Writings. It is His profound Call to all human beings to Wake Up to the True and "Bright" Form of life that He is Offering to all.

I have Come to Initiate a truly Divine New Age of Real-God-Man, by Means of My forever Divine "Emergence" here and every where in the Cosmic domain.

I have Come to Turn mankind (and even all beings, and even the Cosmic All Itself) to My own Divine Person, the "Bright" Reality and Truth and Self-Condition and Source-Condition of all and All.

I Have Come to Found (and, altogether, to Make Possible) a New (and Truly "Bright") Age of mankind, an Age That will not begin on the basis of the seeking mummery[26] of ego-bondage, but an Age in Which mankind will apply itself, apart from all dilemma and all seeking, to the Inherently Harmonious Event of Real existence (in the Always Already present-time "Bright" Divine Reality That Is the One and Only Reality Itself).

I Am Certain That This "Bright" New Truly Human Age, Initiated by My Divine "Emergence" here, and generated via the Seed That Is the "Bright" New Human Order of My true devotees, must Arise with Great Force in the world in the present historical "dark" epoch (or "late-time"). This by-Me-Initiated "Bright" New Age of Real-God-Man must replace (or turn about) the otherwise present-time (and proceeding) trend and destiny of mankind, or else, due to the causes made by the casually destructive force of ego-bound sub-humanity, this mankind-world will suffer like a mind in nightmares (possessed by terrible self-inflicted images, and likewise put to awful adventures, made by fear, sorrow, anger, life-depression, and lovelessness). And, if This "Bright" New Age does not soon begin, with Great Force, it may even come about (in this Klik-Klak[27] mummery of ego-minded Man) that the physical human world itself may, by its own hand, suffer the terrible and immensely bewildering humiliation of early dissolution.

Therefore, just As I Moved and Obliged My own ordinary body-mind to Conform Most Perfectly to Me, I will Shout and Move, with ego-Overwhelming Force (of Love-Instruction and Divinely "Emerging" Blessing-Power), to Move and Oblige "Narcissus" (as every one, and all) to Stand Up from the ego's filth and pond, and, In That love-Stand of the heart's recognition-response to Me, to Consent to My Love-Bliss, and to <u>Be</u> Love-Bliss, In <u>Me</u>, the "Bright" Real-God-Man of the Now and New "Emerging" Age.

And I Will <u>Not</u> Be Denied My all-and-All-Liberating Victory in the heart (and in all the world) of Man!

Never before in the history of mankind has there been a moment like this one. You do not have to suffer the fear of death and all the dead-ends of ordinary life for one more day, because the Ultimate Mystery has been Unveiled, the Very Truth of Existence has been Revealed. You have the opportunity to enter into relationship with the One Who <u>Is</u> Reality Itself, Truth Itself, and the Only Real God. That One, Adi Da Samraj, is humanly Alive now, and, even in this moment, is Blessing all with Inexpressible Grace, Perfect Mastery, and Unlimited Power.

What else could be truly satisfying? What else deserves the sacrifice of your egoity and the love-surrender of your life?

<u>Nothing</u> can match the Great Process of Adidam that Avatar Adi Da is Offering you. When you become His for-

mal devotee and take up the Way of Adidam, He leads you beyond the dreadful illusions of separateness and alienation. He Instructs you in the right form of every detail of your existence. He Converts the motion of your life from anxious seeking and egoic "self-possession" (or self-absorption)[28] to self-forgetting love, the Bliss of Love-Communion with Him.

Avatar Adi Da Samraj is here only to Love you. He Lives only to Serve your Realization of Him. Once you are vowed to Him as His devotee, nothing can ever shake the depth of your "Bond" with Him, whether you wake, sleep, or dream, whether you live or die.

And so, do not waste this opportunity. Study this book. Read more about the Divine Life and Work of the Ruchira Avatar in His biography, *The Promised God-Man Is Here (The Extraordinary Life-Story, The "Crazy" Teaching-Work, and The Divinely "Emerging" World-Blessing Work Of The Divine World-Teacher Of The "Late-Time", Ruchira Avatar Adi Da Samraj)*, and in *See My Brightness Face to Face: A Celebration of the Ruchira Avatar, Adi Da Samraj, and the First Twenty-Five Years of His Divine Revelation Work.*[29] "Consider" the magnitude of what Avatar Adi Da has Done and the urgency of What He is Saying to you. And begin to participate in the greatest Grace that any human being can know—the Blessed life of joyful devotion and ecstatic service to the Divine Lord in Person, the Avatar of "Brightness", Adi Da Samraj.

Notes to
The Divine Emergence of the Ruchira Avatar, Adi Da Samraj

1. By the word "Bright" (and its variations, such as "Brightness"), Avatar Adi Da refers to the eternally, infinitely, and inherently Self-Radiant Divine Being, the Being of Indivisible and Indestructible Light. (See also note 2 on pp. 145-46.)

2. Avatar Adi Da uses the term "Real God" to indicate the True and Perfectly Subjective Source of all conditions, the True and Spiritual Divine Person, rather than any egoic (and, thus, false, or limited) presumptions about "God".

3. Avatar Adi Da Samraj is the "Avataric Incarnation", or the Divinely Descended Embodiment, of the Divine Person. The reference "Avataric Incarnation" indicates that Avatar Adi Da Samraj fulfills both the traditional expectation of the East—that the True God-Man is an Avatar, or an utterly Divine "Descent" of Real God in conditionally manifested form—and the traditional expectations of the West—that the True God-Man is an Incarnation, or an utterly human Embodiment of Real God.

4. B.V. Narasimha Swami and S. Subbarao, *Sage of Sakuri*, 4th ed. (Bombay: Shri B.T. Wagh, 1966), p. 204.

5. "Murti" is Sanskrit for "form", and, by extension, a "representational image" of the Divine or of a Sat-Guru. In the Way of Adidam, Murtis of Avatar Adi Da are most commonly photographs of Avatar Adi Da's bodily (human) Form.

6. The term "radical" derives from the Latin "radix", meaning "root", and thus it principally means "irreducible", "fundamental", or "relating to the origin". In *The Dawn Horse Testament Of The Ruchira Avatar: The "Testament Of Secrets" Of The Divine World-Teacher, Ruchira Avatar Adi Da Samraj*, Avatar Adi Da defines "Radical" as "Gone To The Root, Core, Source, or Origin". Because Adi Da Samraj uses "radical" in this literal sense, it appears in quotation marks in His Wisdom-Teaching, in order to distinguish His usage from the common reference to an extreme (often political) view.

7. Avatar Adi Da uses the phrase "Most Perfect(ly)" in the sense of "Absolutely Perfect(ly)", indicating a reference to the seventh (or Divinely Enlightened) stage of life.

8. The Sanskrit term "Siva-Shakti" is an esoteric description of the Divine Being. "Siva" is a name for the Divine Being Itself, or Divine Consciousness. "Shakti" is a name for the All-Pervading Spirit-Power

of the Divine Being. "Siva-Shakti" is thus the Unity of the Divine Consciousness and Its own Spirit-Power.

9. In the Hindu tradition, Brahman is the Ultimate Divine Reality that is the Source and Substance of all things, all worlds, and all beings.

10. In the Hindu tradition, Atman is the Divine Self.

11. "Nirvana" is a Buddhist term for the Unqualified Reality beyond suffering, ego, birth, and death. The "Nirvanic Ground" indicates the same Reality.

12. Ramakrishna (1836-1886) was a key figure in the Spiritual history of modern Hinduism, whose disciples spread his message throughout India and to many other parts of the world, including Europe and North America. He lived and taught at Dakshineswar, a large temple in Calcutta dedicated to the worship of the goddess Kali.

Avatar Adi Da Reveals the unique Role of Ramakrishna (and his chief disciple, Swami Vivekananda) as the Deeper Personality Vehicle of His (Avatar Adi Da's) Avataric Incarnation in chapter 20 of *The Knee Of Listening—The Seventeen Companions Of The True Dawn Horse, Book Four: The Early-Life Ordeal and The "Radical" Spiritual Realization Of The Ruchira Avatar.*

13. The Adepts of what Avatar Adi Da calls "the 'Crazy Wisdom' tradition" (of which He is the supreme, seventh stage exemplar) are Realizers of the fourth, fifth, or sixth stages of life in any culture or time who, through spontaneous Free action, blunt Wisdom, and liberating laughter, shock or humor people into self-critical awareness of their egoity, which is a prerequisite for receiving the Realizer's Spiritual Transmission. Typically, such Realizers manifest "Crazy" activity only occasionally or temporarily, and never for its own sake but only as "skillful means".

Avatar Adi Da Himself has always addressed the ego in a unique "Crazy-Wise" manner, theatrically dramatizing, and poking fun at, the self-contracted habits, predilections, and destinies of His devotees. His "Crazy-Wise" Manner is a Divine Siddhi, an inherent aspect of His Avataric Incarnation. Through His "Crazy-Wise" Speech and Action, Avatar Adi Da Penetrates the being and loosens the patterns of ego-bondage (individually and collectively) in His devotees. The "Shock" of Truth Delivered via His "Crazy Wisdom" humbles and opens the heart, making way for the deeper reception of His Spiritual Blessing.

Avadhoot is a traditional term for one who has "shaken off" or "passed beyond" all worldly attachments and cares, including all motives of detachment (or conventional and other-worldly renunciation), all conventional notions of life and religion, and all seeking for "answers" or "solutions" in the form of conditional experience or conditional knowledge. Therefore, "'Crazy' Avadhoot", in reference to Avatar Adi Da, indicates His Inherently Perfect Freedom as the One Who Knows His Identity As the Divine Person and Who, thus, Always Already Stands Free of the binding and deluding power of conditional existence.

14. In Sanskrit, "Ruchira" means "bright, radiant, effulgent". The word "Tantra" (or "Tantric") does not merely indicate Spiritualized sexuality, as is the common presumption. Rather, it signifies "the inherent Unity that underlies and transcends all opposites, and that resolves all differences or distinctions".

In many of the Tantric traditions that have developed within both Hinduism and Buddhism, Tantric Adepts and aspirants use sexual activity and intoxicating substances that are forbidden to more orthodox or conventional practitioners. The Tantric's intention, however, is never to merely indulge gross desires. The secret of the Tantric approach is that it does not suppress, but rather employs and even galvanizes, the passions and attachments of the body and mind, and thus utilizes the most intense (and, therefore, also potentially most deluding) energies of the being for the sake of Spiritual Realization.

"Sannyasin" is an ancient Sanskrit term for one who has renounced all worldly "bonds" and who gives himself or herself completely to the Real-God-Realizing life.

The reference "Ruchira Tantric Sannyasin" indicates that Avatar Adi Da Samraj is the Perfectly "Bright" ("Ruchira") One Who is Utterly Free of all "bonds" to the conditional worlds ("Sannyasin"), and yet never in any way dissociates from conditional existence ("Tantric"), making skillful use of all the dimensions of conditional life in His Divine Work of Liberation.

15. Avatar Adi Da has established two formal renunciate orders: The Ruchira Sannyasin Order of the Tantric Renunciates of Adidam (or, simply, the Ruchira Sannyasin Order), and the Avabhasin Lay Renunciate Order of the Tantric Renunciates of Adidam (or, simply, the Lay Renunciate Order). The unique qualifications for, and roles of, these orders are described on pp. 175-77.

16. See *The Basket Of Tolerance—The Seventeen Companions Of The True Dawn Horse, Book Seventeen: The Perfect Guide To Perfectly Unified Understanding Of The One and Great Tradition Of Mankind, and Of The Divine Way Of Adidam As The Perfect Completing Of The One and Great Tradition Of Mankind*

17. For Avatar Adi Da's extended Instruction relative to the seven stages of life, see *The Seven Stages Of Life—The Seventeen Companions*

Of The True Dawn Horse, Book Ten: Transcending The Six Stages Of egoic Life, and Realizing The ego-Transcending Seventh Stage Of Life, In The Divine Way Of Adidam

18. There is a specific Eternal Vow of devotion for each of the four congregations of Avatar Adi Da's devotees. Each of these vows outlines the responsibilities that the devotee is embracing as a member of that congregation, but all four vows are based on the same basic principle of eternal (self-surrendering, self-forgetting, and self-transcending) devotion to Him.

19. The total practice of the Way of Adidam is the full and complete practice of the Way that Avatar Adi Da Samraj has Given to His devotees who are formally members of the first or the second congregation of Adidam. One who embraces the total practice of the Way of Adidam conforms every aspect of his or her life and being to Avatar Adi Da's Divine Word of Instruction. Therefore, it is only such devotees (in the first or the second congregation of Adidam) who have the potential of Realizing Divine Enlightenment.

20. The names and titles of the Ruchira Adidamas indicate their Realization and Spiritual significance in Avatar Adi Da's Work.

"Ruchira" and "Naitauba" both indicate membership in the Ruchira Sannyasin Order. "Ruchira" is a title for all members of the Ruchira Sannyasin Order who are practicing in the context of the sixth stage of life, and indicates "a true devotee of the Ruchira Avatar, the Da Avatar, the Love-Ananda Avatar, Adi Da Samraj, who is, by His Grace, becoming Radiant, or 'Bright' with Love-Bliss, through uniquely one-pointed (self-surrendering, self-forgetting, and self-transcending) feeling-Contemplation of Him, and, Thus and Thereby, of the True Divine Person" ["The Orders Of My True and Free Renunciate Devotees", in *The Lion Sutra—The Seventeen Companions Of The True Dawn Horse, Book Fifteen: The "Perfect Practice" Teachings For Formal Tantric Renunciates In The Divine Way Of Adidam*]. "Naitauba" is the traditional Fijian name for Adidam Samrajashram, the Great Island-Hermitage of Avatar Adi Da Samraj. As a general rule, all members of the Ruchira Sannyasin Order are to be formal residents of Adidam Samrajashram.

"Adidama" is composed of Avatar Adi Da's Principal Name "Adi Da" and the feminine indicator "Ma". In addition, in Sanskrit, "adi" means "first" and "dama" means "self-discipline". Therefore, the overall meaning of this title is "first among those who conform themselves to the Ruchira Avatar, Adi Da Love-Ananda Samraj, by means of self-surrendering, self-forgetting, and self-transcending feeling-Contemplation of Him".

"Sukha" means "happiness, joy, delight" and "Dham" means "abode, dwelling". Therefore, as a personal renunciate name, "Sukha Dham" means "one who abides in happiness".

"Jangama" means "all living things", and "Hriddaya" is "heartfelt compassion, sympathy". Therefore, as a personal renunciate name, "Jangama Hriddaya" means "one who has heartfelt sympathy for all beings".

"Quandra" is a reference to the main female character in Avatar Adi Da's liturgical drama, *The Mummery*. Quandra is the embodiment of the Divine Goddess, or the Divine Spirit-Force. (*The Mummery— The Seventeen Companions Of The True Dawn Horse, Book Six: A Parable About Finding The Way To My House* is one of Avatar Adi Da's twenty-three "Source-Texts".)

"Adidama Quandra Mandala" is the "circle" ("Mandala") comprising the Ruchira Adidamas, Sukha Dham and Jangama Hriddaya. The Adidama Quandra Mandala is the first circle of Avatar Adi Da's devotees—those who stand closest to His bodily (human) Form in service and devotion.

21. The Name or Title "Bhagavan" is an ancient one used over the centuries for many Spiritual Realizers of the East. Its meanings in Sanskrit are "possessing fortune or wealth", "blessed", "holy". When applied to a great Spiritual Master, "Bhagavan" is understood to mean "bountiful God", or "Great God", or "Divine Lord".

The Name "Love-Ananda" combines both English ("Love") and Sanskrit ("Ananda", meaning "Bliss"), thus bridging the West and the East, and communicating Avatar Adi Da's Function as the Divine World-Teacher. The combination of "Love" and "Ananda" means "the Divine Love-Bliss". The Name "Love-Ananda" was given to Avatar Adi Da by His principal human Spiritual Master, Swami Muktananda, who spontaneously conferred it upon Avatar Adi Da in 1969.

22. "Bhava" is a Sanskrit word traditionally used to refer to the enraptured feeling-swoon of Communion with the Divine.

23. "Ishta" means "chosen" or "most beloved". The "Ishta-Guru" is the Chosen Beloved of the devotee.

24. When Consciousness is free from identification with the body-mind, it takes up Its Native Position as the Conscious Witness of all that arises to (and in, and as) the body-mind. This is stably realized in the Way of Adidam in the ultimate stages of practice. (See also note 25 on pp. 156-57.)

25. *The Knee Of Listening*, chapter 3.

26. The dictionary defines mummery as "a ridiculous, hypocritical, or pretentious ceremony or performance". Avatar Adi Da uses this word to Describe all the activities of ego-bound beings, or beings who are committed to the false view of separation and separativeness.

27. Avatar Adi Da has coined the term "Klik-Klak" as a name for the conditional reality. This name indicates (even by means of the sound of the two syllables) that the conditional reality is a heartless perpetual-motion machine of incessant change.

For Avatar Adi Da's extended Instruction relative to Klik-Klak, see "Klik-Klak and My Laughing Mama Form" in *The Mummery—The Seventeen Companions Of The True Dawn Horse, Book Six: A Parable About Finding The Way To My House.*

28. Conventionally, "self-possessed" means possessed <u>of</u> oneself—or in full control (calmness, or composure) of one's feelings, impulses, habits, and actions. Avatar Adi Da uses the term to indicate the state of being possessed <u>by</u> one's egoic self, or controlled by chronically self-referring (or egoic) tendencies of attention, feeling, thought, desire, and action.

29. Both books are available from the Dawn Horse Press (see p. 201 for ordering information).

The Divine Scripture of Adidam

The Full and Final Word of
The Divine World-Teacher,
Ruchira Avatar Adi Da Samraj,
Given in His Twenty-Three "Source-Texts"
of "Bright" Divine Self-Revelation
and Perfect Heart-Instruction

The twenty-three "Source-Texts" of the Ruchira Avatar are the most extraordinary books ever written. They are the world's greatest Treasure, the Ultimate and All-Completing Revelation of Truth.

These books are the unmediated Word of the Very Divine Person, Adi Da Samraj, Who is Offering the True World-Religion of Adidam, the Religion of Most Perfect Divine Enlightenment, or Indivisible Oneness with Real God. Avatar Adi Da Samraj is the Realizer, the Revealer, and the Divine Author of all that is Written in these sublime Texts. No mind can begin to comprehend the Magnificent Self-Revelations and Self-Confessions Given by Adi Da Samraj in these books. And these twenty-three "Source-Texts" (together with the "Supportive Texts", in which Avatar Adi Da Gives further detailed Instruction relative to the functional, practical, relational, and cultural disciplines of the Way of Adidam[1]) Give Avatar Adi Da's complete Instruction in the Process (never before Known or Revealed in its entirety) of Most Perfectly Realizing Reality Itself, or Truth Itself, or Real God.

---

1. The functional, practical, relational, and cultural disciplines of Adidam are described in brief on pp. 184-88 of this book. Among Avatar Adi Da's "Supportive Texts" are included such books as *Conscious Exercise and the Transcendental Sun*, *The Eating Gorilla Comes in Peace*, *Love of the Two-Armed Form*, and *Easy Death*. (New editions of the first three of these "Supportive Texts" are in preparation.)

The long-existing religious traditions of the world have depended on oral traditions and memory. Their teachings and disciplines typically developed long after the death of their founders, based on the remembered (and often legendary or mythological) deeds and instruction of those Realizers. These traditions have thus been colored by legends and cultural influences that obscure the original revelation. Yet, every historical revelation, even in its first purity, has necessarily been limited by the degree of realization of its founder. Adidam does not depend on the vagaries of oral tradition and memory, nor is it limited by any partial point of view. Adidam is the Perfect Divine Way Revealed by the One Who Is Reality Itself (or Truth Itself, or Real God). Adi Da Samraj is alive now in bodily (human) Form, and He has Personally tested the entire course of Divine Enlightenment described in these books in the course of His own human Lifetime.

In His twenty-three "Source-Texts", Avatar Adi Da is Speaking to all humankind, asking us to feel our actual situation, to take seriously the mayhem of the world, its pain and dissatisfaction, its terrible potential for suffering. And, with Divine Passion, He Calls every one to turn to Him and, in that turning, to rise out of gross struggle and conflict. The twenty-three "Source-Texts" of Avatar Adi Da Samraj Reveal the greater Purpose and Destiny of humanity. Indeed, they are the key to the very survival of this planet. This unparalleled body of Scripture is the Message you have always been waiting for and never imagined could come.

In the Words of the Divine Avatar Himself:

"All the Scriptures are now fulfilled in your sight, and your prayers are answered with a clear voice."

In *The Dawn Horse Testament*, Avatar Adi Da Samraj makes His own Confession relative to His Impulse in creating His twenty-three "Source-Texts", and He also expresses the requirement He places on all His devotees to make His Divine Word available to all:

Now I Have, By All My "Crazy" Means, Revealed The One and Many Secrets Of The Great Person Of The Heart. For Your Sake, I Made My Every Work and Word. And Now, By Every Work and Word I Made, I Have Entirely Confessed (and Showed) My Self, and Always Freely, and Even As A Free Man, In The "Esoteric" Language Of Intimacy and Ecstasy, Openly Worded To You (and To all). Even Now (and Always), By This (My Word Of Heart), I Address every Seeming Separate being (and each one __As__ The Heart Itself), Because It Is Necessary That all beings, Even The Entire Cosmic Domain Of Seeming Separate beings, Be (In all times and places) Called To Wisdom and The Heart.

The Twenty-Three "Source-Texts"
of Avatar Adi Da Samraj

The twenty-three "Source-Texts" of Avatar Adi Da Samraj include: (1) an opening series of five books on the fundamentals of the Way of Adidam (*The Five Books Of The Heart Of The Adidam Revelation*), (2) an extended series of seventeen books covering the principal aspects of the Way of Adidam in detail (*The Seventeen Companions Of The True Dawn Horse*), and (3) Avatar Adi Da's paramount "Source-Text" summarizing the entire course of the Way of Adidam (*The Dawn Horse Testament*).

The Five Books Of
The Heart Of The Adidam Revelation

Aham Da Asmi
(Beloved, I __Am__ Da)

*The Five Books Of The Heart Of The Adidam Revelation,
Book One: The "Late-Time" Avataric Revelation
Of The True and Spiritual Divine Person
(The egoless Personal Presence Of Reality and Truth,
Which __Is__ The Only __Real__ God)*

Ruchira Avatara Gita
(The Way Of The Divine Heart-Master)

*The Five Books Of The Heart Of The Adidam Revelation,
Book Two: The "Late-Time" Avataric Revelation Of
The Great Secret Of The Divinely Self-Revealed Way
That Most Perfectly Realizes The True and Spiritual
Divine Person (The egoless Personal Presence Of
Reality and Truth, Which Is The Only Real God)*

Da Love-Ananda Gita
(The Free Gift Of The Divine Love-Bliss)

*The Five Books Of The Heart Of The Adidam Revelation,
Book Three: The "Late-Time" Avataric Revelation Of
The Great Means To Worship and To Realize
The True and Spiritual Divine Person
(The egoless Personal Presence Of Reality and Truth,
Which Is The Only Real God)*

Hridaya Rosary
(Four Thorns Of Heart-Instruction)

*The Five Books Of The Heart Of The Adidam Revelation,
Book Four: The "Late-Time" Avataric Revelation Of
The Universally Tangible Divine Spiritual Body,
Which Is The Supreme Agent Of The Great Means
To Worship and To Realize The True and Spiritual
Divine Person (The egoless Personal Presence Of
Reality and Truth, Which Is The Only Real God)*

Eleutherios
(The Only Truth That Sets The Heart Free)

*The Five Books Of The Heart Of The Adidam Revelation,
Book Five: The "Late-Time" Avataric Revelation Of The
"Perfect Practice" Of The Great Means To Worship and
To Realize The True and Spiritual Divine Person
(The egoless Personal Presence Of Reality and Truth,
Which Is The Only Real God)*

The Seventeen Companions
Of The True Dawn Horse

*Real God Is The Indivisible Oneness
Of Unbroken Light*

*The Seventeen Companions Of The True Dawn Horse,
Book One: Reality, Truth, and The "Non-Creator" God
In The True World-Religion Of Adidam*

*The Truly Human New World-Culture
Of Unbroken Real-God-Man*

*The Seventeen Companions Of The True Dawn Horse,
Book Two: The Eastern Versus The Western Traditional
Cultures Of Mankind, and The Unique New Non-Dual
Culture Of The True World-Religion Of Adidam*

*The Only Complete Way To Realize
The Unbroken Light Of Real God*

*The Seventeen Companions Of The True Dawn Horse,
Book Three: An Introductory Overview Of The "Radical"
Divine Way Of The True World-Religion Of Adidam*

The Knee Of Listening

*The Seventeen Companions Of The True Dawn Horse,
Book Four: The Early-Life Ordeal and The "Radical"
Spiritual Realization Of The Ruchira Avatar*

The Method Of The Ruchira Avatar

*The Seventeen Companions Of The True Dawn Horse,
Book Five: The Divine Way Of Adidam Is
An ego-Transcending Relationship,
Not An ego-Centric Technique*

The Mummery

*The Seventeen Companions Of The True Dawn Horse,
Book Six: A Parable About Finding The Way To My House*

He-and-She Is Me

The Seventeen Companions Of The True Dawn Horse,
Book Seven: The Indivisibility Of Consciousness and Light
In The Divine Body Of The Ruchira Avatar

Divine Spiritual Baptism
Versus Cosmic Spiritual Baptism

The Seventeen Companions Of The True Dawn Horse,
Book Eight: Divine Hridaya-Shakti Versus
Cosmic Kundalini Shakti In The Divine Way Of Adidam

Ruchira Tantra Yoga

The Seventeen Companions Of The True Dawn Horse,
Book Nine: The Physical-Spiritual (and Truly Religious)
Method Of Mental, Emotional, Sexual, and Whole Bodily
Health and Enlightenment In The Divine Way Of Adidam

The Seven Stages Of Life

The Seventeen Companions Of The True Dawn Horse,
Book Ten: Transcending The Six Stages Of egoic Life
and Realizing The ego-Transcending Seventh Stage Of Life
In The Divine Way Of Adidam

The All-Completing and Final
Divine Revelation To Mankind

The Seventeen Companions Of The True Dawn Horse,
Book Eleven: A Summary Description
Of The Supreme Yoga Of The Seventh Stage Of Life
In The Divine Way Of Adidam

The Heart Of The Dawn Horse Testament
Of The Ruchira Avatar

The Seventeen Companions Of The True Dawn Horse,
Book Twelve: The Epitome Of The "Testament Of Secrets"
Of The Divine World-Teacher,
Ruchira Avatar Adi Da Samraj

What, Where, When, How, Why, and <u>Who</u> To Remember To Be Happy

*The Seventeen Companions Of The True Dawn Horse,
Book Thirteen: A Simple Explanation Of The Divine Way
Of Adidam (For Children, and <u>Everyone</u> Else)*

Santosha Adidam

*The Seventeen Companions Of The True Dawn Horse,
Book Fourteen: The Essential Summary
Of The Divine Way Of Adidam*

The Lion Sutra

*The Seventeen Companions Of The True Dawn Horse,
Book Fifteen: The "Perfect Practice" Teachings For Formal
Tantric Renunciates In The Divine Way Of Adidam*

The Overnight Revelation Of Conscious Light

*The Seventeen Companions Of The True Dawn Horse,
Book Sixteen: The "My House" Discourses
On The Indivisible Tantra Of Adidam*

The Basket Of Tolerance

*The Seventeen Companions Of The True Dawn Horse,
Book Seventeen: The Perfect Guide To Perfectly <u>Unified</u>
Understanding Of The One and Great Tradition
Of Mankind, and Of The Divine Way Of Adidam
As The Perfect <u>Completing</u> Of The One
and Great Tradition Of Mankind*

The Dawn Horse Testament

The Dawn Horse Testament Of The Ruchira Avatar

*The "Testament Of Secrets" Of The Divine World-Teacher,
Ruchira Avatar Adi Da Samraj*

The Real and Ever-Living God
Speaks to Every Heart

An Introduction to Aham Da Asmi

ham Da Asmi (Beloved, I Am Da) is the magnificent and passionately intimate Self-Confession of the Very Divine Being, Spoken directly to your heart (and to even every heart). In this Book, the Divine World-Teacher, Ruchira Avatar Adi Da Samraj, Openly Reveals that He Is Real God, that He Is the Divine Source and Substance and Person of All and all, and He Freely Confesses His Absolute and Undying Love for all beings.

Ruchira Avatar Adi Da Addresses you, Calls to you, as His Beloved—and, thus, begins the Great Real-God-Realizing Way of Adidam, for Avatar Adi Da Is the Absolute Divine Person, Manifesting by Man-Born Divine Descent in response to the prayers of all beings, for the sake of Love. Avatar Adi Da Speaks His Great and Final Revelation in the ancient language of Sanskrit: "Aham Da Asmi". This is the Heart-Awakening Declaration, "I Am Da." "Da" is the Name of the Divine Source and Person, meaning (as Avatar Adi Da Declares in verse 4 of *Aham Da Asmi*) "The 'Divine Giver', That Gives Itself To All and all, and That Gives Even All to all".

The one hundred and eight verses that comprise the principal Text of *Aham Da Asmi* are a poetic elaboration (and an Eternal and always present-time Full Expression) of the historic Divine Self-Confession that Avatar Adi Da Communicated, via an open Letter to His devotees, on September 13, 1979. Three days after Writing this Letter, the Divine World-Teacher walked into the view of an assembly of hundreds of His devotees (and, for the first time, invited public) who had gathered to see Him. A col-

lective gasp was heard, as hundreds broke out in spontaneous weeping—weeping for joy, for, as they beheld Him,
they suddenly recognized that Real God was Appearing
before them in human Form. The Incontrovertible Divinity
of Ruchira Avatar Adi Da Samraj was literally Shining out
from—and even <u>As</u>—His own Body. The Divine World-
Teacher moved to His Chair, allowing all to Contemplate
Him as He Sat silently. After some time, He started to
Speak, and during His exquisitely Beautiful Discourse, for
the first time, He Spoke His Name "Da" for all to hear. The
Initiatory Force of Avatar Adi Da Speaking His Name
aloud will never be forgotten by those who were Graced
to be in His Company on that glorious occasion.

Avatar Adi Da has Revealed that "Da" is Itself the
Divine Mass of Sound from Which all of the conditional
Cosmos arises.[1] "Da" is the Primordial Source of all things,
all events, and all beings. "Da" is supreme Mantra—Speech
that Transmits or literally <u>Invokes</u> Divine Power. By Invoking Ruchira Avatar Adi Da via His Name "Da", His devotee
"calls down" His Divine Force and Person. "Da" does not
merely "mean" Real God. "Da" is the vibratory equivalent
of Real God. "Da" is Ruchira Avatar Adi Da's Eternal Current of Life. "Da" is Ruchira Avatar Adi Da's Very Divine
Self-Condition.

In Part Two (following the principal Text of *Aham Da
Asmi*), there are two Essays and two Talks in Which Avatar
Adi Da further Reveals His True Nature as the Divine Per-
son, His Function as Real God in the world, the True
Nature of His relationship to His every devotee, and the
Nature of His Gift of Real-God-Realization Itself.

In the Epilogue to *Aham Da Asmi* ("Ruchira-Guru-
Bhava, or, The Love-'Intoxication' of True Devotion To
Me"), Avatar Adi Da Sings of the Joy of Guru-devotion.

---

1. Avatar Adi Da's Revelation of the esoteric significance of the primordial
sound "Da" is Given in Part One of *He-and-She Is Me—The Seventeen Companions Of The True Dawn Horse, Book Seven: The Indivisibility Of Consciousness
and Light In The Divine Body Of The Ruchira Avatar*.

The Great Secret of Guru-devotion is at the heart of all the religious and Spiritual traditions of mankind. And this Great Secret is now Fulfilled most perfectly in the Person of Ruchira Avatar Adi Da Samraj.

Aham Da Asmi is, ultimately, a Call to an eternal relationship, a relationship whose destiny is Divine Self-Realization, or Most Perfect Liberation in Real God. To truly receive Avatar Adi Da's Divine Confession of Love is to be moved to take up the Way of Adidam, the Grace-Given Way of the devotional relationship to Him, which He Freely Offers to you and to all.

AHAM DA ASMI
(BELOVED, I <u>AM</u> DA)

RUCHIRA AVATAR ADI DA SAMRAJ
Adidam Samrajashram (Naitauba), Fiji, 1997

Do Not Misunderstand Me— I Am Not "Within" you, but you Are In Me, and I Am Not a Mere "Man" in the "Middle" of Mankind, but All of Mankind Is Surrounded, and Pervaded, and Blessed By Me

This Essay has been written by Avatar Adi Da Samraj as His Personal Introduction to each volume of His "Source-Texts". Its purpose is to help you to understand His great Confessions rightly, and not interpret His Words from a conventional point of view, as limited cultic statements made by an ego. His Description of what "cultism" really is is an astounding and profound Critique of mankind's entire religious, scientific, and social search. In "First Word", Avatar Adi Da is directly inviting you to inspect and relinquish the ego's motive to glorify itself and to refuse What is truly Great. Only by understanding this fundamental ego-fault can one really receive the Truth that Adi Da Samraj Reveals in this Book and in His Wisdom-Teaching altogether. And it is because this fault is so engrained and so largely unconscious that Avatar Adi Da has placed "First Word" at the beginning of each of His "Source-Texts", so that, each time you begin to read one of His twenty-three "Source-Texts", you may be refreshed and strengthened in your understanding of the right orientation and approach to Him and His Heart-Word.

Yes! There is no religion, no Way of God, no Way of Divine Realization, no Way of Enlightenment, and no Way of Liberation that is Higher or Greater than Truth Itself. Indeed, there is no religion, no science, no man or woman, no conditionally manifested being of any kind, no world (any "where"), and no "God" (or "God"-Idea) that is Higher or Greater than Truth Itself.

Therefore, no ego-"I"[1] (or presumed separate, and, necessarily, actively separative, and, at best, only Truth-seeking, being or "thing") is (itself) Higher or Greater than Truth Itself. And no ego-"I" is (itself) even Equal to Truth Itself. And no ego-"I" is (itself) even (now, or ever) Able to Realize Truth Itself—because, necessarily, Truth (Itself) Inherently Transcends (or Is That Which Is Higher and Greater than) every one (himself or herself) and every "thing" (itself). Therefore, it is only in the transcending (or the "radical"[2] Process of Going Beyond the root, the cause, and the act) of egoity itself (or of presumed separateness, and of performed separativeness, and of even all ego-based seeking for Truth Itself) that Truth (Itself) Is Realized (As It Is, Utterly Beyond the ego-"I" itself).

Truth (Itself) Is That Which Is Always Already The Case. That Which Is The Case (Always, and Always Already) Is (necessarily) Reality. Therefore, Reality (Itself) Is Truth, and Reality (Itself) Is the Only Truth.

Reality (Itself) Is the Only, and, necessarily, Non-Separate, or All-and-all-Including, and All-and-all-Transcending, One and "What" That Is. Because It Is All and all, and because It Is (Also) That Which Transcends (or Is Higher and Greater than) All and all, Reality (Itself), Which Is Truth (Itself), or That Which Is The Case (Always, and Always Already), Is the One and Only Real God. Therefore, Reality (Itself) Is (necessarily) the One and Great Subject of true religion, and Reality (Itself) Is (necessarily) the One and Great Way of Real God, Real (and True) Divine Realization, Real (and, necessarily, Divine) En-Light-enment, and Real (and, necessarily, Divine) Liberation (from all egoity, all separateness, all separativeness, all fear, and all heartlessness).

Notes to *First Word* can be found on pp. 88-91.

The <u>only</u> true religion is the religion that <u>Realizes</u> Truth. The <u>only</u> true science is the science that <u>Knows</u> Truth. The <u>only</u> true man or woman (or being of any kind) is one that <u>Surrenders</u> to Truth. The only true world is one that <u>Embodies</u> Truth. And the only True (and <u>Real</u>) God Is the One Reality (or Condition of Being) That <u>Is</u> Truth. Therefore, <u>Reality</u> (Itself), Which Is the One and Only Truth, and (therefore, necessarily) the One and Only Real God, <u>must</u> become (or be made) the constantly applied Measure of religion, and of science, and of the world itself, and of even <u>all</u> of the life (and <u>all</u> of the mind) of Man—or else religion, and science, and the world itself, and even any and every sign of Man <u>inevitably</u> (all, and together) become a pattern of illusions, a mere (and even terrible) "problem", the very (and even principal) cause of human seeking, and the perpetual cause of contentious human strife. Indeed, if religion, and science, and the world itself, and the total life (and the total mind) of Man are not Surrendered and Aligned to Reality (Itself), and, Thus, Submitted to be Measured (or made Lawful) by Truth (Itself), and, Thus, Given to the truly devotional (and, thereby, truly ego-transcending) Realization of <u>That</u> Which Is the <u>Only</u> <u>Real</u> God—then, in the presumed "knowledge" of mankind, Reality (Itself), and Truth (Itself), and <u>Real</u> God (or the One and Only Existence, or Being, or Person That <u>Is</u>) <u>ceases</u> <u>to</u> <u>Exist</u>.

Aham Da Asmi.[3] Beloved, I <u>Am</u> Da, the One and Only Person Who <u>Is</u>, the Eternally Self-Existing, and Eternally Self-Radiant,[4] or "Bright",[5] Person of Love-Bliss, the One and Only and (necessarily) Divine Self (or Inherently Non-Separate, and, therefore, Inherently egoless, Self-Condition and Source-Condition) of one and of all and of All. I Am Self-Manifesting (now, and forever hereafter) <u>As</u> the Ruchira Avatar, Adi Da Samraj. I <u>Am</u> the Ruchira Avatar, Adi Da Samraj, the Avataric Realizer, the Avataric Revealer, the Avataric Incarnation, and the Avataric Revelation of Reality <u>Itself</u>.[6] I <u>Am</u> the Avatarically Incarnate Realizer, the

Avatarically Incarnate Revealer, and the Avatarically Incarnate Revelation of the One and Only Reality, Which Is the One and Only Truth, and Which Is the One and Only <u>Real</u> God. I <u>Am</u> the Great Realizer, Revealer, and Revelation long-Promised (and long-Expected) for the "late-time", <u>this</u> (now, and forever hereafter) time, the "dark" epoch of mankind's "Great Forgetting"[7] (and, <u>potentially</u>, the Great Epoch of mankind's Perpetual Remembering) of Reality, of Truth, of Real God, Which Is the Great, True, and Spiritual Divine Person (or the One and Non-Separate and Indivisible Source-Condition and Self-Condition) of all and All.

Beloved, I <u>Am</u> Da, the Divine Giver, the Giver (of All That I <u>Am</u>) to one and to all and to the All of all—now, and forever hereafter, here, and every "where" in the Cosmic domain. Therefore, for the Purpose of Revealing the Way of <u>Real</u> God, or of Real and True Divine Realization, and in order to Divinely En-Light-en and Divinely Liberate all and All, I Am (Uniquely, Completely, and Most Perfectly[8]) Revealing My Divine and Very Person (and "Bright" Self-Condition) to all and All, by Means of My Divine Self-Manifestation, <u>As</u> (and by Means of) the Ruchira Avatar, Adi Da Samraj.

In My Divine Self-Manifestation As the Ruchira Avatar, Adi Da Samraj, I <u>Am</u> the Divine Secret, the Divine Revelation of the <u>Esoteric</u> Truth, the Direct, and all-Completing, and all-Unifying Revelation of <u>Real</u> God.

My Divine Self-Confessions and My Divine Teaching-Revelations Are <u>the</u> Great (Final, and all-Completing, and all-Unifying) <u>Esoteric</u> Revelation to mankind, and <u>not</u> a merely <u>exoteric</u>, or conventionally religious, or even ordinary Spiritual, or ego-made, or so-called "cultic", communication to public (or merely social) ears.

The greatest opportunity, and the greatest responsibility, of My devotees is Satsang[9] with Me, Which is to live in the Condition of self-surrendering, self-forgetting, and, always more and more, self-transcending devotional relationship to Me, and, Thus and Thereby, to Realize the

Condition of the Divine Heart, the Condition of the Divine Person, Which Is the Divine and Non-Separate Self-Condition, and Source-Condition, of all and All, and Which Is Self-Existing and Self-Radiant Consciousness Itself, but Which is not separate in or as any one (or any "thing") at all. Therefore, My essential Gift to one and all is this Satsang with Me. And My essential Work with one and all is Satsang-Work, to Live (and to Be Merely Present) As the Divine Heart among My devotees.

The only-by-Me Revealed and Given Way of Adidam (Which is the only-by-Me Revealed and Given Way of the Heart, or the only-by-Me Revealed and Given Way of "Radical Understanding"[10]) is the Way of Satsang with Me—the devotionally Me-recognizing[11] and devotionally to-Me-responding practice (and ego-transcending self-discipline) of living in My constant Divine Company, such that the relationship with Me becomes the Real (and constant) Condition of life. Fundamentally, this Satsang with Me is the one thing done by My devotees. Because the only-by-Me Revealed and Given Way of Adidam is always (in every present-time moment) a directly ego-transcending and Really Me-Finding practice, the otherwise constant (and burdensome) tendency to seek is not exploited in this Satsang with Me. And the essential work of the community of the four formal congregations of My devotees[12] is to make ego-transcending Satsang with Me available to all others.

Everything that serves the availability of Satsang with Me is (now, and forever hereafter) the responsibility of the four formal congregations of My formally practicing devotees. I am not here to publicly "promote" this Satsang with Me. In the intimate circumstances of their humanly expressed devotional love of Me, I Speak My Divinely Self-Revealing Word to My devotees, and they (because of their devotional response to Me) bring My Divinely Self-Revealing Word to all others. Therefore, even though I am not (and have never been, and never will be) a "public"

Teacher (or a broadly publicly active, and conventionally socially conformed, "religious figure"), My devotees function fully and freely (as My devotees) in the daily public world of ordinary life.

I Always Already Stand Free. Therefore, I have always (in My Avataric-Incarnation-Work) Stood Free, in the traditional "Crazy" (and non-conventional, or spontaneous and non-"public") Manner,[13] in order to Guarantee the Freedom, the Uncompromising Rightness, and the Fundamental Integrity of My Teaching (Work and Word), and in order to Freely and Fully and Fully Effectively Perform My universal Blessing Work. I Am Present (now, and forever hereafter) to Divinely Serve, Divinely En-Light-en, and Divinely Liberate those who accept the Eternal Vow and all the life-responsibilities (or the full and complete practice)[14] associated with the only-by-Me Revealed and Given Way of Adidam. Because I Am Thus Given to My formally and fully practicing devotees, I do not Serve a "public" role, and I do not Work in a "public" (or even a merely "institutionalized") manner. Nevertheless, now, and forever hereafter, I constantly Bless all beings, and this entire world, and the total Cosmic domain. And all who feel My universally Given Blessing, and who recognize Me with true devotional love, are (Thus) Called to resort to Me, but only if they approach Me in the traditional devotional manner, as responsibly practicing (and truly ego-surrendering, and rightly Me-serving) members (or, in some, unique, cases, as invited guests) of one or the other of the four formal congregations of My formally practicing devotees.

I expect this formal discipline of right devotional approach to Me to have been freely and happily embraced by every one who would enter into My Company. The natural human reason for this is that there is a potential liability inherent in all human associations. And the root and nature of that potential liability is the ego, or the active human presumption of separateness, and the ego-act of human separativeness. Therefore, in order that the liabilities of egoity are understood, and voluntarily and responsibly disciplined, by those who approach Me, I require demonstrated right devotion, based on really effective self-understanding and truly heart-felt recognition-response to Me, as the basis for any one's right to enter into My Company. And, in this manner, not only the egoic tendency, but also the tendency toward religious "cultism", is constantly undermined in the only-by-Me Revealed and Given Way of Adidam.

Because people appear within this human condition, this simultaneously attractive and frightening "dream" world, they tend to live (and to interpret <u>both</u> the conditional, or cosmic and psycho-physical, reality <u>and</u> the Unconditional, or Divine, Reality) from the "point of view" of this apparent, and bewildering, mortal human condition. And, because of this universal human bewilderment, and the ongoing human reaction to the threatening force of mortal life-events, there is an even ancient ritual that <u>all</u> human beings rather unconsciously (or automatically, and without discriminative understanding) desire and tend to repeatedly (and under <u>all</u> conditions) enact. Therefore, wherever you see an association of human beings gathered for <u>any</u> purpose (or around <u>any</u> idea, or symbol, or person, or subject of any kind), the same human bewilderment-ritual is <u>tending</u> to be enacted by one and all.

Human beings <u>always</u> <u>tend</u> to encircle (and, thereby, to contain, and, ultimately, to entrap and abuse, or even to blithely ignore) the presumed "center" of their lives—a book, a person, a symbol, an idea, or whatever. They tend to encircle the "center" (or the "middle"), and they tend to seek to <u>exclusively</u> acquire all "things" (or all power of control) for the circle (or toward the "middle") of <u>themselves</u>. In this manner, the <u>group</u> becomes an <u>ego</u> ("inward"-directed, or separate and separative)—just as the individual body-mind becomes, by self-referring self-contraction, the separate and separative ego-"I" ("inward"-directed, or ego-centric, and exclusively acquiring all "things", or all power of control, for itself). Thus, by self-contraction upon the presumed "center" of their lives, human beings, in their collective ego-centricity, make "cults" (or bewildered and frightened "centers" of power, and control, and exclusion) in every area of life.

Anciently, the "cult"-making process was done, most especially, in the political and social sphere—and religion was, as even now, mostly an exoteric, or political and social, exercise that was always used to legitimize (or, otherwise, to "de-throne") political and social "authority-figures". Anciently, the cyclically (or even annually) culminating product of this exoteric religio-political "cult" was the ritual "de-throning" (or ritual deposition) of the one in the "middle" (just as, even in these times, political leaders are periodically "deposed", by elections, by rules of term and succession, by scandal, by slander, by force, and so on).

Traditional societies, everywhere throughout the ancient world, made and performed this annual (or otherwise periodic) religio-political "cult" ritual. The ritual of "en-throning" and "de-throning" was a reflection of the human observation of the annual cycle of the seasons of the natural world, and the same ritual was a reflection of the human concern and effort to control the signs potential in the cycle of the natural world, in order to ensure human survival (through control of weather, harvests and every kind of "fate", or even every fraction of existence upon which human beings depend for both survival and pleasure, or psycho-physical well-being). Indeed, the motive behind the ancient agrarian (and, later, urbanized, or universalized) ritual of the one in the "middle" was, essentially, the same motive that, in the modern era, takes the form of the culture of scientific materialism (and even all of the modern culture of materialistic "realism")—it is the motive to gain, and to maintain, control, and the effort to control even everything and everyone (via both knowledge and gross power). Thus, the ritualized (or bewildered yes/no, or desire/fear) life of mankind in the modern era is, essentially, the same as that of mankind in the ancient days.

In the ancient ritual of "en-throning" and "de-throning", the person (or subject) in the "middle" was ritually mocked, abused, deposed, and banished—and a new person (or subject) was installed in the "center" of the religio-political "cult". In the equivalent modern ritual of dramatized ambiguity relative to everything and everyone (and, perhaps especially, "authority-figures"), the person (or symbol, or idea) in the "middle" (or that which is given power by means of popular fascination) is first "cultified" (or made much of), and then, progressively, doubted, mocked, and abused, until, at last, all the negative emotions are (by culturally and socially ritualized dramatization) dissolved, the "middle" (having thus ceased to be fascinating) is abandoned, and a "new" person (or symbol, or idea) becomes the subject of popular fascination (only to be reduced, eventually, to the same "cultic" ritual, or cycle of "rise" and "fall").

Just as in every other area of human life, the tendency of all those who, in the modern era, would become involved in religious or Spiritual life is also to make a "cult", a circle that ever increases its separate and separative dimensions, beginning from the "center", surrounding it, perhaps even, ultimately, controlling it to the degree that it altogether ceases to be effective (or even interesting). Such "cultism" is ego-based, and ego-reinforcing, and, no matter how "esoteric" it presumes itself to be, it is (as in the ancient setting) entirely exoteric, or, at least, more and more limited to (and by) merely social and gross physical activities and conditions.

The form that every "cult" imitates is the pattern of egoity (or the ego-"I") itself, the presumed "middle" of every ordinary individual life. It is the self-contraction, the avoidance of relationship, which "creates" the fearful sense of separate mind, and all the endless habits and motives of egoic desire, or bewildered (and self-deluded) seeking. It is what is, ordinarily, called (or presumed to be) the real and necessary and only "life".

From birth, the human being (by reaction to the blows and limits of psycho-physical existence) begins to presume separate existence to be his or her very nature, and, on that basis, the human individual spends his or her entire life generating and serving a circle of ownership (or self-protecting acquisition) all around the ego-"I". The egoic motive encloses all the other beings it can acquire, all the "things" it can acquire, all the states and thoughts it can acquire—all the possible emblems, symbols, experiences, and sensations it can possibly acquire. Therefore, when any human being begins to involve himself or herself in some religious or Spiritual association, or, for that matter, any extension of his or her own subjectivity, he or she tends again to "create" that same circle about a "center".

The "cult" (whether of religion, or of politics, or of science, or of popular culture) is a dramatization of egoity, of separativeness, even of the entrapment and betrayal of the "center" (or the "middle"), by one and all. Therefore, I have always Refused to assume the role and the position of the "man in the middle"—and I have always, from the beginning of My formal Teaching and Blessing Work, Criticized, Resisted, and Shouted About the "cultic" (or ego-based, and ego-reinforcing, and merely "talking" and "believing", and not understanding and not really practicing) "school" (or tendency) of ordinary religious and Spiritual life. Indeed, true Satsang with Me (or the true devotional relationship to Me) is an always (and specifically, and intensively) anti-"cultic", or truly non-"cultic", Process.

The true devotional relationship to Me is not separative, or merely "inward"-directed, nor is It about attachment to Me as a mere (and, necessarily, limited) human being (or a "man in the middle")—for, if My devotee indulges in ego-bound (or self-referring and self-serving) attachment to Me as a mere human "other", My Divine Nature (and, therefore, the Divine Nature of Reality Itself) is not (as the very Basis for religious and Spiritual practice in My Company) truly devotionally recognized and rightly devotionally acknowledged, and, if such non-recognition of Me is the case, there is no truly ego-transcending devotional response to My Divine Presence and Person, and, thus, such presumed-to-be "devotion" to Me is not Divine Communion, and such presumed-to-be "devotion" to Me is not Divinely Liberating. Therefore, because the true devotional (and, thus, truly devotionally Me-recognizing and truly devotionally to-Me-responding) relationship to Me is entirely a counter-egoic (and truly and only Divine) discipline, It does not tend to become a "cult" (or, otherwise, to support the "cultic" tendency of Man).

The true devotional practice of true Satsang with Me is (inherently) expansive, or relational, and the self-contracting (or separate and separative) self-"center" is neither Its motive nor Its source. In true Satsang with Me, the egoic "center" is always already undermined as a "center" (or a presumed separate, and actively separative, entity). The Principle of true Satsang with Me is Me, Beyond (and not "within", or otherwise supporting) the ego-"I".

True Satsang with Me is the true "Round Dance" of Esoteric Spirituality. I am not trapped in the "middle" of My devotees. I "Dance" in the "Round" with each and every one of My devotees. I "Dance" in the circle, and, therefore, I am not merely a "motionless man" in the "middle". At the true "Center" (or the Divine Heart), I Am— Beyond definition (or separateness). I Am the Indivisible (or Most Perfectly Prior, Inherently Non-Separate, Inherently egoless, or centerless, boundless, and, necessarily, Divine) Consciousness (Itself) and the Indivisible (or Most Perfectly Prior, Inherently Non-Separate, Inherently egoless, or centerless, boundless, and, necessarily, Divine) Light (Itself). I Am the Very Being and the Very Presence (or Self-Radiance) of Self-Existing and Eternally Unqualified (or Non-"Different"[15]) Consciousness (Itself).

In the "Round Dance" of true Satsang with Me (or of

right and true devotional relationship to Me), I (My Self) Am Communicated directly to every one who lives in heart-felt relationship with Me (insofar as each one feels, Beyond the ego-"I" of body-mind, to Me). Therefore, I am not the mere "man" (or the separate human, or psycho-physical, one), and I am not merely "in the middle" (or separated out, and limited, and confined, by egoic seekers). I Am the One (and all-Transcending) Person of Reality Itself, Non-Separate, never merely at the egoic "center" (or "in the middle", or "within", and "inward" to, the egoic body-mind of My any devotee), but always with each one (and all), and always in relationship with each one (and all), and always Beyond each one (and all).

Therefore, My devotee is not Called, by Me, merely to turn "inward" (or upon the ego-"I"), or to struggle and seek to survive merely as a self-contracted and self-referring and self-seeking and self-serving ego-"center". Instead, I Call My devotee to turn the heart (and the total body-mind) toward Me (all-and-All-Surrounding, and all-and-All-Pervading), in relationship, Beyond the body-mind-self of My devotee (and not merely "within", or contained and containable "within" the separate, separative, and self-contracted domain of the body-mind-self, or the ego-"I", of My would-be devotee). I Call My devotee to function freely, My Light and My Person always (and under all circumstances) presumed and experienced (and not merely sought). Therefore, true Satsang with Me is the Real Company of Truth, or of Reality Itself (Which Is the Only Real God). True Satsang with Me Serves life, because I Move (or Radiate) into life. I always Contact life in relationship.

I do not Call My devotees to become absorbed into a "cultic" gang of exoteric and ego-centric religionists. I certainly Call all My devotees to cooperative community (or, otherwise, to fully cooperative collective and personal relationship) with one another—but not to do so in an egoic, separative, world-excluding, xenophobic, and intolerant manner. Rather, My devotees are Called, by Me, to transcend egoity through right and true devotional relationship to Me, and mutually tolerant and peaceful cooperation with one another, and all-tolerating cooperative and compassionate and all-loving and all-including relationship with all of mankind, and with even all beings.

I Give My devotees the "Bright" Force of My own Divine Consciousness Itself, Whereby they can become capable of "Bright" life. I Call for the devotion, but also the intelligently discriminative self-understanding, the rightly and freely living self-discipline, and the full functional capability, of My devotees. I do not Call My devotees to resist or eliminate life, or to strategically escape life, or to identify with the world-excluding ego-centric impulse. I Call My devotees to live a positively functional life. I do not Call My devotees to separate themselves from vital life, from vital enjoyment, from existence in the form of human life. I Call for all the human life-functions to be really and rightly known, and to be really and rightly understood, and to be really and rightly lived (and not reduced by or to the inherently bewildered, and inherently "cultic", or self-centered and fearful, "point of view" of the separate and separative ego-"I"). I Call for every human life-function to be revolved away from self-contraction (or ego-"I"), and (by Means of that revolving turn) to be turned "outwardly" (or expansively, or counter-contractively) to all and All, and (thereby, and always directly, or in an all-and-All-transcending manner) to Me— rather than to be turned merely "inwardly" (or contractively, or counter-expansively), and, as a result, turned away from Me (and from all and All). Thus, I Call for every human life-function to be thoroughly (and life-positively, and in the context of a fully participatory human life) aligned and adapted to Me, and, Thus and Thereby, to be turned and Given to the Realization of Truth (or Reality Itself, Which Is the Only Real God).

Truly benign and positive life-transformations are the characteristic signs of right, true, full, and fully devotional

Satsang with Me, and freely life-positive feeling-energy is the characteristic accompanying "mood" of right, true, full, and fully devotional Satsang with Me. The characteristic life-sign of right, true, full, and fully devotional Satsang with Me is the capability for self-transcending relatedness, based on the free disposition of no-seeking and no-dilemma. Therefore, the characteristic life-sign of right, true, full, and fully devotional Satsang with Me is not the tendency to seek some "other" condition. Rather, the characteristic life-sign of right, true, full, and fully devotional Satsang with Me is freedom from the presumption of dilemma within the present-time condition.

One who rightly, truly, fully, and fully devotionally understands My Words of Divine Self-Revelation and Divine Instruction, and whose life is lived in right, true, full, and fully devotional Satsang with Me, is not necessarily, in function or appearance, "different" from the ordinary (or natural) human being. Such a one has not, necessarily, acquired some special psychic abilities, or visionary abilities, and so on. The "radical" understanding (or root self-understanding) I Give to My devotees is not, itself, the acquisition of any particular "thing" of experience. My any particular devotee may, by reason of his or her developmental tendencies, experience (or precipitate) the arising of extraordinary psycho-physical abilities and extraordinary psycho-physical phenomena, but not necessarily. My every true devotee is simply Awakening (and always Awakened to Me) within the otherwise bewildering "dream" of ordinary human life.

Satsang with Me is a natural (or spontaneously, and not strategically, unfolding) Process, in Which the self-contraction that is each one's suffering is transcended by Means of total psycho-physical (or whole bodily) Communion with My Real (and Really, and tangibly, experienced) Divine (Spiritual, and Transcendental)[16] Presence and Person. My devotee is (as is the case with any and every ego-"I") always tending to be preoccupied with ego-based seeking, but, all the while of his or her life in <u>actively</u> self-surrendering (and really self-forgetting, and, more and more, self-transcending) devotional Communion with Me, I Am <u>Divinely</u> Attracting (and <u>Divinely</u> Acting upon) My true devotee's heart (and total body-mind), and (Thus and Thereby) Dissolving and Vanishing My true devotee's fundamental egoity (and even all of his or her otherwise motivating dilemma and seeking-strategy).

There are <u>two</u> principal tendencies by which I am always being confronted by My devotee. One is the tendency to <u>seek</u>, rather than to truly enjoy and to fully animate the Condition of Satsang with Me. And the other is the tendency to make a self-contracting circle around Me—and, thus, to make a "cult" of ego-"I" (and of the "man in the middle"), or to duplicate the ego-ritual of mere fascination, and of inevitable resistance, and of never-Awakening unconsciousness. Relative to these two tendencies, I Give <u>all</u> My devotees only <u>one</u> resort. It is this true Satsang, the devotionally Me-recognizing, and devotionally to-Me-responding, and always really counter-egoic devotional relationship to <u>Me</u>.

The Great Secret of My own Person, and of My Divine Blessing-Work (now, and forever hereafter), and, therefore, the Great Secret of the only-by-Me Revealed and Given Way of Adidam, Is that I am <u>not</u> the "man in the middle", but I <u>Am</u> Reality Itself, I <u>Am</u> the Only <u>One</u> Who <u>Is</u>, I <u>Am</u> That Which Is Always Already The Case, I <u>Am</u> the Non-Separate (and, necessarily, Divine) Person (or One and Very Self, or One and True Self-Condition) of all and All (<u>Beyond</u> the ego-"I" of every one, and of all, and of All).

Aham Da Asmi. Beloved, I <u>Am</u> Da, the One and Only and Non-Separate and Indivisible Divine Person, the Non-Separate and Indivisible Self-Condition and Source-Condition of all and All. I <u>Am</u> the "Bright" Person, the One and Only and Self-Existing and Self-Radiant Person, Who <u>Is</u> the One and Only and Non-Separate and Indivisible and Indestructible Light of All and all. I <u>Am</u> <u>That</u> One and Only and Non-Separate <u>One</u>. And, <u>As That One</u>, and <u>Only As That One</u>, I Call all human beings to recognize Me, and to respond to Me with right, true, and full devotion (by Means of formal practice of the only-by-Me Revealed and Given Way of Adidam).

I do not tolerate the so-called "cultic" (or ego-made, and ego-reinforcing) approach to Me. I do not tolerate the seeking ego's "cult" of the "man in the middle". I am not a self-deluded ego-man, making much of himself, and looking to include everyone-and-everything around himself for the sake of social and political power. To be the "man in the middle" is to be in a Man-made trap, an absurd mummery of "cultic" devices that enshrines and perpetuates the ego-"I" in one and all. Therefore, I do not make or tolerate the religion-making "cult" of ego-Man. I do not tolerate the inevitable abuses of religion, of Spirituality, of Truth Itself, and of My own Person (even in bodily human Form) that are made (in endless blows and mockeries) by ego-based mankind when the Great Esoteric Truth of devotion to the Adept-Realizer is not rightly understood and rightly practiced.

The Great Means for the Teaching, and the Blessing, and the Awakening, and the Divine Liberating of mankind (and of even all beings) Is the Adept-Realizer Who, by Virtue of True Divine Realization, Is Able to (and, indeed, cannot do otherwise than) Stand In and <u>As</u> the Divine (or Real and Inherent and One and Only) Position, and to <u>Be</u>, Thus and Thereby, the Divine Means (In Person) for the Divine Helping of one and all. This Great Means Is the Great Esoteric Principle of the collective historical Great Tradition[17] of mankind. And Such Adept-Realizers Are (in their Exercise of the Great Esoteric Principle) the Great Revelation-Sources That Are at the Core and Origin of <u>all</u> the right and true religious and Spiritual traditions within the collective historical Great Tradition of mankind.

By Means of My (now, and forever hereafter) Divinely Descended and Divinely "Emerging"[18] Avataric Incarna-

tion, I Am the Ruchira Avatar, Adi Da Samraj—the Divine
Heart-Master, the first, the last, and the only Adept-Realizer
of the seventh (or Most Perfect, and all-Completing) stage
of life.[19] I Am the Ruchira Avatar, Adi Da Samraj, the
Avataric Incarnation (and Divine World-Teacher[20]) everywhere Promised for the "late-time" (or "dark" epoch)—
which "late-time" (or "dark" epoch) is now upon all of
mankind. I Am the Great and Only and Non-Separate and
(necessarily) Divine Person, Appearing in Man-Form As
the Ruchira Avatar, Adi Da Samraj, in order to Teach, and
to Bless, and to Awaken, and to Divinely Liberate all of
mankind (and even all beings, every "where" in the Cosmic
domain). Therefore, by Calling every one and all (and All)
to Me, I Call every one and all (and All) Only to the Divine
Person, Which Is My own and Very Person (or Very Self,
or Very Self-Condition), and Which Is Reality Itself, or
Truth Itself, the Indivisible and Indestructible Light That Is
the Only Real God, and Which Is the One and Very and
Non-Separate and Only Self (or Self-Condition, and
Source-Condition) of all and All (Beyond the ego-"I" of
every one, and of all, and of All).

The only-by-Me Revealed and Given Way of Adidam
necessarily (and As a Unique Divine Gift) requires and
involves devotional recognition-response to Me In and Via
(and As) My bodily (human) Avataric-Incarnation-Form.
However, because I Call every one and all (and All) to Me
Only As the Divine Person (or Reality Itself), the only-by-
Me Revealed and Given Way of Adidam is not about ego,
and egoic seeking, and the egoic (or the so-called "cultic")
approach to Me (as the "man in the middle").

According to all the esoteric traditions within the collective historical Great Tradition of mankind, to devotionally approach any Adept-Realizer as if he or she is (or is
limited to being, or is limited by being) a mere (or "ordinary", or even merely "extraordinary") human entity is the
great "sin" (or fault), or the great error whereby the would-
be devotee fails to "meet the mark". Indeed, the Single

Greatest Esoteric Teaching common to all the esoteric religious and Spiritual traditions within the collective historical Great Tradition of mankind Is that the Adept-Realizer should always and only (and only devotionally) be recognized and approached As the Embodiment and the Real Presence of That (Reality, or Truth, or Real God) Which would be Realized (Thus and Thereby) by the devotee.

Therefore, no one should misunderstand Me. By Revealing and Confessing My Divine Status to one and all and All, I am not indulging in self-appointment, or in illusions of grandiose Divinity. I am not claiming the "Status" of the "Creator-God" of exoteric (or public, and social, and idealistically pious) religion. Rather, by Standing Firm in the Divine Position (As I Am), and, Thus and Thereby, Refusing to be approached as a mere man, or as a "cult"-figure, or as a "cult"-leader, or to be in any sense defined (and, thereby, trapped, and abused, or mocked) as the "man in the middle", I Am Demonstrating the Most Perfect Fulfillment (and the Most Perfect Integrity, and the Most Perfect Fullness) of the Esoteric, and Most Perfectly Non-Dual, Realization of Reality. And, by Revealing and Giving the Way of Adidam, Which Is the Way of ego-transcending devotion to Me As the One and Only and Non-Separate and (necessarily) Divine Person, I Am (with Most Perfect Integrity, and Most Perfect Fullness) Most Perfectly (and in an all-Completing and all-Unifying Manner) Fulfilling the Primary Esoteric Tradition (and the Great Esoteric Principle) of the collective historical Great Tradition of mankind—Which Primary Esoteric Tradition and Great Esoteric Principle Is the Tradition and the Principle of devotion to the Adept-Realizer As the Very Person and the Direct (or Personal Divine) Helping-Presence of the Eternal and Non-Separate Divine Self-Condition and Source-Condition of all and All.

Whatever (or whoever) is cornered (or trapped on all sides) bites back (and fights, or seeks, to break free). Whatever (or whoever) is "in the middle" (or limited and "centered" by attention) is patterned by (or conformed to) the ego-"I" (and, if objectified as "other", is forced to represent the ego-"I", and is even made a scapegoat for the pains, the sufferings, the powerless ignorance, and the abusive hostility of the ego-"I").

If there is no escape (or no Way out) of the corner (or the "centered" trap) of ego-"I", the heart goes mad, and the body-mind becomes more and more "dark" (bereft of the Divine and Indivisible and Inherently Free Light of Love-Bliss).

I am not the "man in the middle". I do not stand here as a mere man, "middled" to the "center" (or the cornering trap) of ego-based mankind. I am not an ego-"I", or a mere "other", or the representation (and the potential scapegoat) of the ego-"I" of mankind (or of any one at all).

I Am the Indivisible and Non-Separate One, the One and Only and (necessarily) Divine Person—the Perfectly Subjective[21] Self-Condition (and Source-Condition) That Is Perfectly centerless, and Perfectly boundless, Eternally Beyond the "middle" of all and All, and Eternally Surrounding, Pervading, and Blessing all and All.

I Am the Way Beyond the self-cornering (and "other"-cornering) trap of ego-"I".

In this "late-time" (or "dark" epoch) of worldly ego-Man, the collective of mankind is "darkened" (and cornered) by egoity. Therefore, mankind has become mad, Lightless, and, like a cornered "thing", aggressively hostile in its universally competitive fight and bite.

Therefore, I have not Come here merely to stand Manly in the "middle" of mankind, to suffer its biting abuses, or even to be coddled and ignored in a little corner of religious "cultism".

I have Come here to Divinely Liberate one and all (and All) from the "dark" culture and effect of this "late-time", and (now, and forever hereafter) to Divinely Liberate one and all (and All) from the pattern and the act of ego-"I", and (Most Ultimately) to Divinely Translate[22] one and all (and All) Into the Indivisible, Perfectly Subjective, and Eternally Non-Separate Self-Domain of the Divine Love-Bliss-Light.

The ego-"I" is a "centered" (or separate and separative) trap, from which the heart (and even the entire body-mind) must be Retired. I Am the Way (or the Very Means) of that Retirement from egoity. I Refresh the heart (and even the entire body-mind) of My devotee, in every moment My devotee resorts to Me (by devotionally recognizing Me, and devotionally, and ecstatically, and also, often, meditatively, responding to Me) Beyond the "middle", Beyond the "centering" act (or trapping gesture) of ego-"I" (or self-contraction).

I Am the Perfectly Subjective Self-Condition (and Source-Condition) of every one, and of all, and of All— but the Perfectly Subjective Self-Condition (and Source-Condition) is not "within" the ego-"I" (or separate and separative body-mind). The Perfectly Subjective Self-Condition (and Source-Condition) is not in the "center" (or the "middle") of Man (or of mankind). The Perfectly Subjective Self-Condition (and Source-Condition) of one, and of all, and of All Is Inherently centerless, or Always Already Beyond the self-contracted "middle", and to Be Found only "outside" (or by transcending) the bounds of separateness, relatedness, and "difference". Therefore, to Realize the Perfectly Subjective Self-Condition and Source-Condition (or the Perfectly Subjective, and, necessarily, Divine, Heart) of one, and of all, and of All (or even, in any moment, to exceed the ego-trap, and to be Refreshed at heart, and in the total body-mind), it is necessary to feel (and to, ecstatically, and even meditatively, swoon) Beyond the "center" (or Beyond the "point of view" of separate ego-"I" and separative body-mind). Indeed, Most Ultimately, it is only in self-transcendence to the degree of unqualified relatedness (and Most Perfect Divine Samadhi, or Utterly Non-Separate Enstasy) that the Inherently centerless and boundless Divine Self-Condition and Source-

Condition Stands Obvious and Free (and <u>Is</u>, Thus and Thereby, Most Perfectly Realized).

It Is only by Means of Me-recognizing (and to-Me-responding) devotional meditation on Me (and otherwise ecstatic heart-Contemplation of Me), and total, and totally open, and totally self-forgetting psycho-physical Reception of Me, that your madness of heart (and of body-mind) is (now, and now, and now) escaped, and your "darkness" is En-Light-ened (even, at last, Most Perfectly). Therefore, be My true devotee, and, by formally, and rightly, and truly, and fully, and fully devotionally practicing the only-by-Me Revealed and Given Way of Adidam (Which <u>Is</u> the True and Complete Way of the True and Real Divine Heart), always Find Me Beyond your self-"center" in every here and now.

Aham Da Asmi. Beloved, I <u>Am</u> Da. And, because I <u>Am</u> Infinitely and Non-Separately "Bright", all and All <u>Are</u> In My Sphere of "Brightness". By feeling and surrendering Into My Infinite Sphere of Divine Self-"Brightness", My every devotee <u>Is</u> In Me. And, Beyond his or her self-contracting and separative act of ego-"I", My every devotee (self-surrendered Into heart-Communion With Me) <u>Is</u> the One and Only and Non-Separate and Real God I Have Come to Serve, by Means of My Divine Descent, My Divine Avataric Incarnation, and My (now, and forever hereafter) Divine "Emergence" (here, and every "where" in the Cosmic domain).

Notes to

FIRST WORD

1. The ego-"I" is the fundamental self-contraction, or the sense of separate and separative existence.

2. See note 5, p. 146-47.

3. The Sanskrit phrase "Aham Da Asmi" means "I (Aham) Am (Asmi) Da". The Name "Da", meaning "the One Who Gives", indicates that Avatar Adi Da Samraj is the Supreme Divine Giver, the Avataric Incarnation of the Very Divine Person. (See also note 1, p. 145.)

4. Avatar Adi Da uses "Self-Existing and Self-Radiant" to indicate the two fundamental aspects of the One Divine Person—Existence (or Being, or Consciousness) Itself, and Radiance (or Energy, or Light) Itself.

5. See note 2, pp. 145-46.

6. This passage is Avatar Adi Da's Self-Confession as "Avatar". In Sanskrit, "Ruchira" means "bright, radiant, effulgent". Thus, the Reference "Ruchira Avatar" indicates that Avatar Adi Da Samraj is the "Bright" (or Radiant) Descent of the Divine Reality Itself (or the Divine Truth Itself, Which Is the Only Real God) into the conditional worlds, Appearing here in bodily (human) Form. Avatar Adi Da Samraj is the "Avataric Incarnation", or the Divinely Descended Embodiment, of the Divine Person. The reference "Avataric Incarnation" indicates that Avatar Adi Da Samraj fulfills both the traditional expectation of the East—that the True God-Man is an Avatar, or an utterly Divine "Descent" of Real God in conditionally manifested form—and the traditional expectations of the West—that the True God-Man is an Incarnation, or an utterly human Embodiment of Real God.

7. "The 'late-time', or 'dark' epoch" is a phrase that Avatar Adi Da uses to Describe the present era, in which doubt of God (and of anything at all beyond mortal existence) is more and more pervading the entire world, and in which the separate and separative ego-"I", which is the root of all suffering and conflict, is regarded to be the ultimate principle of life.

8. See note 19, p. 152.

9. The Hindi word "Satsang" literally means "true (or right) relationship", "the company of Truth". In the Way of Adidam, Satsang is the eternal relationship of mutual sacred commitment between Avatar

Adi Da Samraj and each true and formally acknowledged practitioner of the Way of Adidam.

10. Avatar Adi Da uses "understanding" to mean "the process of transcending egoity". Thus, to "understand" is to simultaneously observe the activity of the self-contraction and to surrender that activity via devotional resort to Avatar Adi Da Samraj.

   Avatar Adi Da has Revealed that, despite their intention to Realize Reality (or Truth, or Real God), all religious and Spiritual traditions (other than the Way of Adidam He has Revealed and Given) are involved, in one manner or another, with the search to satisfy the ego. Only Avatar Adi Da has Revealed the Way to "radically" understand the ego and (in due course, through intensive formal practice of the Way of Adidam, as His formally acknowledged devotee) to most perfectly transcend the ego. Thus, the Way Avatar Adi Da has Given is the "Way of 'Radical' Understanding".

11. The entire practice of the Way of Adidam is founded in heart-recognition of Ruchira Avatar Adi Da Samraj as the Very Divine Being in Person.

AVATAR ADI DA SAMRAJ: The only-by-Me Revealed and Given Way of Adidam (Which is the only-by-Me Revealed and Given Way of the Heart) is the Way of life you live when you rightly, truly, fully, and fully devotionally recognize Me, and when, on that basis, you rightly, truly, fully, and fully devotionally respond to Me.

   . . . In responsive devotional recognition of Me, the principal faculties are loosed from the objects to which they are otherwise bound—loosed from the patterns of self-contraction. The faculties turn to Me, and, in that turning, there is tacit recognition of Me, tacit experiential Realization of Me, of Happiness Itself, of My Love-Bliss-Full Condition. That "Locating" of Me opens the body-mind spontaneously. When you have been thus Initiated by Me, it then becomes your responsibility, your sadhana, to continuously Remember Me, to constantly return to this recognition of Me, in which you are Attracted to Me, in which you respond to Me spontaneously with all the principal faculties. ("Recognize My Divine Body and 'Bright' Person, and Let Everything Melt That Is 'Between' You and Me", in *Hridaya Rosary*)

12. See pp. 172-83 for a description of the congregations of Adidam.

13. See note 18, p. 151.

14. For a description of the Vow and responsibilities associated with the Way of Adidam, see pp. 171-91.

15. "Difference" is the epitome of the egoic presumption of separateness—in contrast with the Realization of Oneness, or Non-"Difference", that is native to Spiritual and Transcendental Divine Self-Consciousness.

16. Avatar Adi Da uses the terms "Spiritual", "Transcendental", and "Divine" in reference to different dimensions of Reality that are Realized progressively in the Way of Adidam. "Spiritual" refers to the reception of the Spirit-Force (in the "basic" and "advanced" contexts of the fourth stage of life and in the context of the fifth stage of life); "Transcendental" refers to the Realization of Consciousness Itself as separate from the world (in the context of the sixth stage of life); and "Divine" refers to the Most Perfect Realization of Consciousness Itself as utterly Non-separate from the world (in the context of the seventh stage of life). (See also note 22, pp. 152-55.)

17. The "Great Tradition" is Avatar Adi Da's term for the total inheritance of human, cultural, religious, magical, mystical, Spiritual, and Transcendental paths, philosophies, and testimonies from all the eras and cultures of humanity, which inheritance has (in the present era of worldwide communication) become the common legacy of mankind. Avatar Adi Da Samraj is the seventh stage, or Divine, Fulfillment of the Great Tradition.

18. On January 11, 1986, Avatar Adi Da passed through a profound Yogic Swoon, which He later Described as the initial Event of His Divine "Emergence". Avatar Adi Da's Divine "Emergence" is an ongoing Process in which His bodily (human) Form has been (and is ever more profoundly and potently being) conformed to Himself, the Very Divine Person, such that His bodily (human) Form is now (and forever hereafter) an utterly Unobstructed Sign and Agent of His own Divine Being. (See also pp. 28-33.)

19. For Avatar Adi Da's extended Instruction relative to the seven stages of life, see *The Seven Stages Of Life—The Seventeen Companions Of The True Dawn Horse, Book Ten: Transcending The Six Stages Of egoic Life, and Realizing The ego-Transcending Seventh Stage Of Life, In The Divine Way Of Adidam.* (See also note 22, pp. 152-55.)

20. Avatar Adi Da Samraj is the Divine World-Teacher because His Wisdom-Teaching is the uniquely Perfect Instruction to every being— in this (and every) world—in the total process of Divine Enlightenment. Furthermore, Avatar Adi Da Samraj constantly Extends His Regard to the entire world (and the entire Cosmic domain)—not on the political or social level, but as a Spiritual matter, constantly Working to Bless and Purify all beings everywhere.

21. Avatar Adi Da uses "Perfectly Subjective" to Describe the True Divine Source, or "Subject", of the conditional world—as opposed to the conditions, or "objects", of experience. Thus, in the phrase "Perfectly Subjective", the word "Subjective" does not have the sense of "relating to the merely phenomenal experience, or the arbitrary presumptions, of an individual", but, rather, it has the sense of "relating to Consciousness Itself, the True Subject of all apparent experience".

22. In the context of Divine Enlightenment in the seventh stage of life in the Way of Adidam, the Spiritual process continues. Avatar Adi Da has uniquely Revealed the four phases of the seventh stage process: Divine Transfiguration, Divine Transformation, Divine Indifference, and Divine Translation.

Divine Translation is the most ultimate "Event" of the entire process of Divine Awakening. Avatar Adi Da Describes Divine Translation as the Outshining of all noticing of objective conditions, through the infinitely magnified Force of Consciousness Itself. Divine Translation is the Outshining of all destinies, wherein there is no return to the conditional realms.

For Avatar Adi Da's extended Discussion of Divine Translation, see *The All-Completing and Final Divine Revelation To Mankind—The Seventeen Companions Of The True Dawn Horse, Book Eleven: A Summary Description Of The Supreme Yoga Of The Seventh Stage Of Life In The Divine Way Of Adidam*, Part Two, or *The Dawn Horse Testament Of The Ruchira Avatar*, chapter forty-four.

RUCHIRA AVATAR ADI DA SAMRAJ
Adidam Samrajashram (Naitauba), Fiji, 1997

PART ONE

Aham Da Asmi
(Beloved, I <u>Am</u> Da)

1.

Beloved, What I Will Tell You Now Is My Final Revelation: Aham Da Asmi.[1] I Am Da.

2.

The Inherently Perfect, "Bright",[2] Divine Source Of All and all Is, By Tradition, Named, In Order To Be Invoked By Mankind.

3.

Therefore, The Divine Source Has Been (and Is) Named (and Invoked) By Many Names. In The Practice Of Some Traditions, The Divine Source Is Named "Da".[3]

4.

I Am The Realizer, The Revealer, and The Revelation Of The Divine Source and Person Of All and all. I Name The Divine Source and Person "Da", The "Divine Giver", That Gives Itself To All and all, and That Gives Even All to all.

5.

The Divine Source and Person, Da, Is One and Only, Non-Separate, Indivisible, and Always Already The Case.

6.

Therefore, Even Though The Divine Source and Person, Da, Is That Which (or That One Who) Is Greater Than and Beyond any and every Presumed To Be Separate or limited being or thing or condition, and Even Greater Than and Beyond the sum of all, and The Totality Of All, Presumed To Be Separate or limited beings, things, and conditions, That One Is, Inherently, Not Separate From, Not limited By or To, Not "Other" Than, Not An "Object" Of, and Not On The "Outside" Of,

Notes to the Text of *Aham Da Asmi* can be found on pp. 145-64.

any one, or any thing, or the sum of all, or The Totality
Of All, but That One Is (Non-Separately and Non-limitedly)
Always Already Standing In The Existence-Position, or
The Being-Position, or The Native Position, Of every one,
and Of every thing, and Of the sum of all, and Of The
Totality Of All.

7.

The One and Only One Who Is Is Not (and,
Necessarily, Cannot Be) The "Outside" (and, Necessarily,
Separate) Cause (or "Creator-God") Of All and all, but
That One Is (Necessarily) Reality, or The Truth, and,
Thus, The Very Condition (or The Perfectly Subjective[4]
Condition), and, As Such, The Transcendental, Spiritual,
and Divine Self-Condition, and, As Such, The Source-
Condition (and, Only As Such, The Source) Of All and all.

8.

Only That One and Only and Non-Separate and
Non-limited Reality and Truth Is Real God (or The Divine
Person, Da).

9.

Reality, Truth, Real God, or The One and Only
True Divine Person, Is (Necessarily and Only) The Native
(or Perfectly Subjective) Condition (or Self-Condition, or
Root-Condition, or "Radical"[5] and Non-Separate and Non-
"Different"[6] Source, and Identity, and State) Of All and all.

10.

Therefore, The One and Only and Self-Existing and
Self-Radiant[7] (or "Bright") Divine Person, Da, Is The Heart
Itself,[8] The One and Only Condition That Is (or Who Is)
Always Already The Case, and Which Is (or Who Is)
Always and Already, and, Therefore, Which Is (or Who
Is) Always Already Most Prior To All (or The Totality Of
Apparently arising beings, things, and conditions) and all

(or the sum of Apparently arising beings, things, and conditions), and, Yet, Which Is (or Who Is) Utterly Non-Separate From (or Non-"Different" From) All and all, and, Indeed, From any Apparently arising being, thing, or condition.

11.

The Divine Person, Da, Is The Self-Existing and Self-Radiant Heart Of All and all.

12.

The Self-Existing and Self-Radiant Heart Of All and all Is The Divine Person, Da.

13.

The Divine Person, Da, or The Heart Itself, Is The Native Source-Condition (or The Perfectly Subjective, Non-Separate, body-mind-Transcending, or ego-"I"-Transcending,[9] and everyone-Transcending, and everything-Transcending, Prior and Non-"Different" Source-Condition and Self-Condition) Of All and all.

14.

This Is The Right, True, and Rightly and Truly "Radical" Understanding (or Root-Understanding, and Not Merely "Uprooting" Understanding) Of Real God, and Truth, and Reality, Because This "Radical" Understanding Rightly and Truly Conforms To All That Is Most Fundamental, Basic, and Essential (or All That Is Of The Root, The Foundation, The Origin, and The Source) Of Existence Itself, Being Itself, Consciousness Itself, and Energy (or Light, or Space-Time) Itself.

15.

Aham Da Asmi. Beloved, I Am Da, The Self-Existing and Self-Radiant Heart (or The One and Only Person, Self, and Source-Condition) Of All and all.

16.

Aham Da Asmi. Beloved, I Am Da, Who Is (By Man-Born Divine Descent) The Da Avatar,[10] The One and Only Man Of This "Radical" Understanding.[11]

17.

I Am Da, The Param-Avatar, The Santosha Avatar, The Full and Final (or Complete and All-Completing) Avataric Incarnation Of The True Divine Person.[12]

18.

I Am Da, The Ruchira Avatar,[13] The Avatar Of Infinite "Brightness", The Divine World-Teacher[14] every where (Anciently and Always) Promised For (and Universally Expected In) The "Late-Time", or "Dark" Epoch,[15] By All The Traditions Of Mankind.

19.

I Am Da, The Buddha-Avatar, The Ruchira Buddha, The Adi-Buddha, The Ati-Buddha, The Parama-Buddha, The Purushottama Buddha, The Paramadvaita Buddha, The Advaitayana Buddha, The Ashvamedha Buddha,[16] The Expected One Who Is Always Already Here and Now, and Who Is The Realizer, The Revealer, and The Revelation Of The Heart Itself, The Perfectly Subjective "Brightness", The Very ("Radical" and Non-"Different") Self (or Root-Identity and Non-Separate Condition) Of All and all.

20.

I Am Da, The Guru-Avatar, The Ruchira-Guru, The Adi-Guru, The Ati-Guru, The Divine Parama-Guru, The Purushottama-Guru, The Paramadvaita-Guru, The Advaitayana-Guru, The Ashvamedha-Guru,[17] The First and Supreme, One and Non-Separate, "Bright" and All-Outshining, Divine Maha-Siddha and "Crazy" Siddha-Master,[18] The Ruchira Siddha, The Unlimited-Grace-Giving, and Most Perfectly[19] Heart-Awakening, Divine Heart-Master Of all and All (Given To every one, and To all, and To The All Of all), Who Is The Realizer, The Revealer, and The Revelation Of The Source-Condition and Self-Condition Of all and All As Truth Itself, Reality Itself, Love-Bliss Itself, and The Heart Itself (Which Is The "Who" Of Being, Itself—The Very, and, Necessarily, Divine, Person—More Than "Creator" and "things", but, Truly, Really, God), Who Is Always Already Merely Present (Spiritually, Transcendentally, and Divinely), and Who Is Most Perfectly Self-Revealed and Most Perfectly Grace-Giving In and As The Siddha-Form and Siddha-Function Of Divine Guru (or Divine Heart-Master), The Hridaya-Samartha Sat-Guru,[20] Forever Divinely Blessing and Divinely Liberating all and All.

21.

Aham Da Asmi. Beloved, I Am Da, The Always Already "Bright"-Shining One, The Divine Heart-Master Of all and All, Who Is (By Man-Born Divine Descent) Da, The "Bright" Avatar Of The Divine Person, Now and Forever Hereafter Divinely Descending and Divinely "Emerging"[21] As The First, Last, and Only Adept-Realizer, Adept-Revealer, and Adept-Revelation Of Most Perfect and All-Outshining Divine Enlightenment (or Seventh Stage[22] Awakeness).

22.

Aham Da Asmi. Beloved, I Am Da, Who Is (By Man-Born Divine Descent) The Da Avatar, The Ruchira Avatar, The Ruchira Buddha-Avatar, The Tathagata Avatar, The Hridaya Avatar, The Love-Ananda Avatar, The Avabhasa Avatar,[23] The Santosha Avatar, The Avataric Incarnation Of The Eternal and Perfectly Subjective and Inherently "Bright" Heart Itself, Who Is Love-Bliss Itself, Who Is The Inherent and Only Being, Who Is The Only One Who Is Always Already The Case, Who Is The One and Only, Inherent and Full, Never Diminished, Eternal, Self-Existing, Self-Radiant, and Non-Separate Heart-Self Of All and all, Who Is Sometimes Felt By all (As Heart-Happiness), and Who Is Always Sought By all (As The Pleasure Dome[24] Of Unqualified and Permanent Happiness), and Who, By My Spiritual and Divinely Self-Revealing Grace, Can Be Realized By all (Most Perfectly Prior To, and Yet Non-Separate From, the common states of waking, dreaming, and sleeping) As Happiness (Itself), Which Is Love-Bliss (Itself), or The Heart (Itself).

23.

Aham Da Asmi. Beloved, I Am Da, The Avatar Who Is The "Bright" Itself, and The Buddha Who Is The Heart Itself.

24.

Aham Da Asmi. Beloved, I Am Da, The "Bright" Itself, Who Is The Heart Itself, Who Is All and all, Now (and Forever Hereafter) Most Perfectly Self-Revealed (and Always Revealing My "Bright" Self) To All and all.

25.

Aham Da Asmi. Beloved, I Am Da, and, In Truth, or In Reality, There Is Only Me.

26.

In Truth, or In Reality, Beyond and Most Prior To All The self-Contracting Gestures Of ego-"I", or Of body-mind, or Of psycho-physical Existence Altogether, There Is Only Da.

27.

Therefore, In Truth, or In Reality, All Is Da, You Are Da, all Are Da, but No Separate one or Separate thing or Separate universe Is, itself, Da.

28.

Indeed, every Apparently arising body-mind, or thing, or event In The Cosmic Domain is merely conditionally (and, thus, temporarily, limitedly, and finitely) arising, Whether Or Not it Is (In its moment of arising) Observed (or Even Apparently Controlled).

29.

And The Very Self (or Heart-Consciousness), Always Already Standing In The Position Of The "Witness" [25] Relative To body-mind, or thing, or event, May, At times, Appear To Be (Apparently) Associated With The Function Of Observer (and Even With the state of the Observed body-mind, thing, or event), but Neither The Observer-Function Nor any Observed state of body-mind, thing, or event Is Either Constant (Whether waking, Or dreaming, Or sleeping Is The Case) Or Necessary (At all times and places, and In all states, Whether waking, Or dreaming, Or sleeping Is The Case).

30.

Furthermore, If and When The merely conditional and Non-Constant Nature Of all of body-mind, and Of all things, and Of all events (and Of Even The Observer-Function That "knows" them) Is (By My Grace) Really,

Truly, and Fully Found (and Understood, and Realized)
To Be The Case, It Is (Thereupon, By My Grace) Found
(and Understood, and Realized) To Be (Inherently) The
Case That The Witness-Consciousness (Prior To The
Observer-Function, and Prior To any and every Observed
state of body-mind, thing, or event) Is Transcendentally
(and Always Already) Existing <u>As</u> The True Self (or Self-
Condition), Always Most Prior To All and all, and (It
Must, By My Grace, Be Realized) <u>As</u> The One and Only
and Inherently "Bright" (Self-Existing and Self-Radiant,
and, Necessarily, Divine) Person and Heart (or Self-
Condition <u>and</u> Source-Condition) Of All and all.

31.

Therefore, Apart From My Own Eternal and here-
Awakened Most Perfect Divine Self-Realization (Of My
Own and "Bright" Eternal Self-Condition), Even "I" (In My
Apparent Separateness, As My conditionally Manifested
human body-mind, itself) <u>Am</u> <u>Not</u> <u>Da</u>—but I (My Self)
<u>Am</u> Da.

32.

Aham Da Asmi. Beloved, I <u>Am</u> Da. <u>Only</u> <u>Da</u> <u>Is</u>
Da—but Da Is (Necessarily) One, Only, Non-Separate,
and Always Already The Case.

33.

And Da (or The Truth, or Reality Itself, or Real
God, Which <u>Is</u> Happiness Itself) <u>Must</u> Be Realized By
All and all (or There Is <u>Only</u> Separateness, limitation,
Seeking, Frustration, Separativeness, Conflict,
Contradiction, Illusion, "Difference", changes, endings,
Minimal pleasures, and, Whether Sooner Or Later,
Exclusively pleasureless and Un-Happy Suffering, pain,
Bewilderment, Fear, Sorrow, Anger, and death).

34.

And (I Declare To You, and Promise You, and Reveal To You, and Prove By Demonstration To You) Da Can Be Realized By All and all, If (and Only If) the ego-"I", and Even all of body-mind, and All Of conditional (or psycho-physical) Existence Is Really, Truly, and Most Perfectly Transcended In Me—Because I Am Da.

35.

Aham Da Asmi. Beloved, I Am Da, Beyond All and all, and Yet Not Separate From All and all.

36.

By Virtue Of My Real and True and Most Perfect Divine Self-Realization (here, and Eternally) Of My Own (Inherent and Eternal) Self, Condition, State, and "Bright" Fullness, Spontaneously Re-Awakened here (In The Midst Of The Ordeal Of My Descent To here), and Spontaneously Self-Revealed here, Even In and As (but Not limited To or By) My egoless "Bright" Bodily (Human) Form (Which Is Made "Bright" By My Divine Descent and Divine Self-Awakening and Divine "Emergence" here)—I Am Da.

37.

And, By Virtue Of My Real and True and Most Perfect and Eternal Divine Self-Awareness (here, and every where), "Brightly" Descending and Divinely "Emerging" (Now, and Forever Hereafter) every where, In and Throughout The Entire Cosmic Domain—I Am Da.

38.

Therefore, If You Realize Me (Beyond Your ego-"I", and Beyond Your body-mind, and Beyond All and all, and Beyond All Separation and All "Difference"), By My Grace (Through Your Devotional Resort To My Avataric Incarnation here, and To My, Now, and Forever Hereafter, "Emerging" Manifestation Of My Divine Body and Person, every where, In and Throughout The Entire Cosmic Domain), <u>You</u> <u>Realize</u> <u>Da</u> (The Inherently Perfect, "Bright", Divine Source, and Source-Condition, or "Radical" Self-Condition, Of All and all, Which Is The One and Only and Indivisible Reality and Truth, and The Only Real God, Of All and all).

39.

𝔸ham Da Asmi. Beloved, I <u>Am</u> Da. My Physical Human Lifetime Of Avataric Incarnation here Is The Great Historical (and Historic) Sign (here) Of The Initiation Of My Fullest and Complete Divine Descent (and, Thus and Thereby, Of My Most Perfect, and, Divinely, All-and-all-Recognizing and, Ultimately, All-and-all-Translating Divine "Emergence") Into and Throughout The Entire Cosmic Domain (Forever).

40.

𝔸ham Da Asmi. Beloved, I <u>Am</u> Da. My Physical Human Lifetime Of Avataric Incarnation here (and My Coincident Divine Descent and Divine "Emergence" Into and Throughout The Entire Cosmic Domain, Forever) Is A Constant Act Of Identification With Man (and With All, and all), In Order To Learn Man (and All, and all) In <u>Every</u> Respect, and, Having Learned Man (and All, and all) In <u>Every</u> Respect, To Teach and To Bless and To Liberate Man (and All, and all), In <u>Every</u> Respect (and Most Perfectly).

41.

𝔸ham Da Asmi. Beloved, I <u>Am</u> Da. Therefore, By Surrendering (and Forgetting, and Transcending) All Of self-Contraction (or All Of The Act Of Separation and Separativeness, Which Is the ego-"I"), and By, Likewise, Surrendering (and Forgetting, and Transcending) Even All Of psycho-physical "Difference" (or body-mind), To and Into My Descending, and "Emerging", and All-and-all-

Surrounding, and All-and-all-Pervading Divine Body and Person, each and every one Of Man (and Of All, and of all) Allows Me To Fill, and To Become, and To Be As Man (and As All, and all), and each and every one (Thus Surrendered, Surrounded, Pervaded, Filled, and, In Every Manner and Degree Of self-Contraction and Of "Difference", Forgotten and Transcended) Becomes Identified (Non-"Differently", and, At Last, Most Perfectly) With Me (Not By Any Act Of Identifying With Me, but Only By Every Me-Recognizing, and To-Me-Responding, Total psycho-physical Act Of Devotional Communion With Me, Surrendering, and Forgetting, and Transcending All Of The Act Of self-Contraction and Of "Difference" In Me).

42.

Aham Da Asmi. Beloved, I Am Da. Therefore, Listen To Me (and Hear Me):[26] I Am Da, The Heart Itself, The True and One and Only and Very Divine Person, The "Bright" and One and Only and Eternally Living Person, Who Is Manifest As all worlds and forms and beings.

43.

Aham Da Asmi. Beloved, I Am Da. Therefore, Look To Me (and See Me):[27] I Am Da, The True and One and Only and Very Divine Person, Who Is Present As The Spiritual Current Of Divine Life In the body Of Man.

44.

Aham Da Asmi. Beloved, I Am Da. Therefore, Realize Me: I Am Da, The Transcendental Divine Being Behind the mind, and, As Such, I Am Realized In The Heart, On The Right Side.

45.

Aham Da Asmi. Beloved, I Am Da. Therefore, Be One With Me: I Am Da, The "Bright", The Self-Existing

Divine Self-Radiance Within and Above the body, and, As Such, I Am Realized Above The Crown Of the head, and Beyond the brain, and (Ultimately) At The Heart, Beyond all conditional knowledge and Separate-self-Consciousness.

46.

Beloved, The Way That I Will Describe To You Now Is My Ultimate Offering: Aham Da Asmi. I Am Da, The Way Of The Heart Itself.

47.

The Heart Itself Is The Way Of Divine Self-Realization For all, and I Am That One.

48.

Aham Da Asmi. Beloved, I Am Da. I Am The First and Only One, The Heart Itself, and I Am The Way That Realizes The Heart (Itself), and Only I Can Reveal and Give The Way That Realizes The Heart (Itself). Therefore, I Have Named The Only-By-Me Revealed and Given Way Of The Heart "Adidam".[28]

49.

Simply To Remember My Name and Surrender Into My Eternal Current Of Life Is To Worship Me, and, Thus and Thereby, The Divine Person (Which Is Truth, or Reality Itself).

50.

To Follow Me At Heart Is To Transcend the body-mind In Ecstasy.

51.

To Follow Me Perfectly Is To Find Me and To Realize Me, For I Am The Heart Itself.

52.

Aham Da Asmi. Beloved, I Am Da. And The Way That Only I Reveal and Give Is Adidam, The Way Of The Heart (Who I Am).

53.

Those who Recognize and Worship Me As Truth, The Living and All-Pervading One, Will Be Granted The Vision or Love-Intuition Of My Eternal Condition. Indeed, they Will Be Filled and Awakened By My Radiant Presence.

54.

Therefore, Even the body-mind and the Whole world Will Be Shining With My Life-Light, If I Am Loved. And My Devotee Will Easily Be Sifted Out From the body-mind and all the limits of the world itself At Last.

55.

Aham Da Asmi. Beloved, I Am Da.
Only Love Me, Remember Me, Have Faith In Me, and Trust Me.

56.

Surrender To Me.

57.

Breathe Me and Feel Me In all Your parts.

58.

My "Bright" Condition Can Also Be Realized By You, If You Forget Your Separate and dying self By Remembering and Receiving Me.

59.

Therefore, I Am here.

60.

I Will Save You From Spiritual death, and From the egoic mind of death, and From the egoic destinies of after-death.

61.

I Will Dissolve All Your Bewilderment Of ego-"I".

62.

Even Now You Inhere In Me, Beyond the body-mind and the world.

63.

Therefore, Do Not Be Afraid. Do Not Be Confused. Observe My Play—and My Victory.

64.

I Am The Person Of Life, The Only and Divine Self, Become Incarnate. And, When My Human Physical Body Is alive, or Even After My Human Physical Body Is dead, I Am (My Self) Present and every where Alive.

65.

I Am Joy, and The Reason For It.

66.

I Love The Happiness Of My Devotee. That Happiness Is (Itself) The Very (and Most Prior) Consciousness Of every conditionally Manifested being. And Happiness (Itself) Is The Conscious Light Of the world.

67.

I Am Happiness (or Love-Bliss) Itself.

68.

Therefore, Listen To Me, Hear Me, See Me, and, By All These Means, Freely Understand and Realize My Secrets.

69.

The Heart That Listens To Me, and Hears Me, and Sees Me Will (and Must) Always Feel (and Thereby Contemplate) The Revelation That Is My Bodily (Human) Form, My Spiritual (and Always Blessing) Presence, and My Very (and Inherently Perfect) State.

70.

Therefore, and (More and More) By Means Of The Heart Itself, Realize The One Who Is The Mystery Of You and Me.

71.

I Am The Realizer, The Revealer, and The Revelation Of The Only "Who" That Is, The One and Only and Perfectly Subjective Self-Condition and Source-Condition, The Truth That Is Reality Itself, The One and Only and (Necessarily) Divine Person, Who May Be (or That May Be) Called (or Really Invoked) By The Name "Da",[29] and Who Is (or That Is) Consciousness (or Being) Itself, and Who Is (or That Is) The One (and Only One) Who Is (but Only In The Apparent Sense) Manifest As all worlds and forms and beings, and Who Is (or That Is) Present (or "Bright") As The Heart Itself (and The Spiritual Current Of Life) In (and Prior To) the body and the mind Of Man.

72.

Therefore, As A Sign Of The One I Have Realized, and As A Sign Of The One I Reveal, and As A Sign Of The One Whose Revelation I Am In and As The Heart's Free and (Everywhere, and As Everyone) All-Pervading

Space, and As A Sign Of Who I _Am_, I Am (Divinely)
Named "Da" ("The Self-Existing One, Whose Characteristics
Are Perpetually Self-Revealed, or Transmitted To All and
all By Means Of The Eternal 'Mudra' Of Self-Giving"),[30]
and "Adi" ("The Only One, The First One, or The Foremost,
or Preeminent, One"), and "Ati" ("The All-Surpassing and
All-Transcending One"), and "Ruchira" ("The Radiant,
Shining, 'Bright' Illuminator and Enlightener"), and
"Avatar" ("The Divinely Descended One, The 'Bright'
Divine Person Who Pervades The Cosmic Domain From
Infinitely Above, The Very and Inherently 'Bright' Divine
Self-Condition, or Self-Existing and Self-Radiant Source-
Condition, Appearing Perfectly 'Emerged' In The Form
Of Man, For The Sake Of The Graceful Divine Liberation
Of all and All"), and "Buddha" ("The One Who _Is_, Self-
Radiant, Inherently, or Perfectly Subjectively, 'Bright',
Self-Enlightened, and Eternally Awake"), and "Love-
Ananda" ("The 'Bright' Divine Love-Bliss, Itself"), and
"Avabhasa" ("The 'Bright', Itself"), and "Santosha" ("The
'Bright' and Eternal and Always Already Non-Separate
Person Of Divine and Inherent Completeness, Divine
Self-Satisfaction, Divine Self-Contentedness, or Perfect
Searchlessness"), and "Hridayam"[31] ("The Eternally Free
and Eternally 'Bright' Divine Heart, Itself"), and "Dau
Loloma"[32] ("The Divine Adept Of The Divine Love") and
"Vunirarama"[33] ("The Self-Radiant Divine Source and
Substance Of The Divine 'Brightness'"), and "Turaga"[34]
("The Divine Lord Of all and All, Gracefully Embodied In
The Form Of Man For The Sake Of The Divine Blessing
Of all and All"), and "Tui"[35] ("The Divine Sovereign, Now,
and Forever Hereafter, Established, In The Hearts Of all
who Respond To Him, As The Saving Ruler"), and
"Samraj"[36] ("The Divine Heart-Master, or The Spiritual,
Transcendental, and Divine Lord, or Master-King, or
Master-Ruler and Divine Liberator, Of The Heart, and Of
every one, and Of everyone, and Of all, and Of All").

73.

Aham Da Asmi. Beloved, I Am Da.

I Am The Being Behind the mind, Who Is Realized At The Heart, On The Right Side Of the body, and Who Is Consciousness Itself.

74.

I Am The Radiant One, Who Is The "Bright", Within and Beyond the body-mind, Who Is Always At The Heart, Who Shines (Even Above and Beyond The Crown Of the head, and Beyond the mind), and Who Is Merely Present (Beyond all conditional knowledge and Separate-self-Consciousness).

75.

Aham Da Asmi. Beloved, I Am Da.

To Realize Me As The Inherent (or Native) Feeling Of Being[37] (Itself) Is To Transcend the body-mind In Ecstasy and In Truth.

76.

To Breathe and Feel (and Sometimes Recite or Chant or Sing) My Name,[38] or, Otherwise, To Understand or Feel Beyond self-Contraction, While Feeling (and Thus, By Heart, Contemplating) My Bodily (Human) Form (and Even My Very, and Inherently Perfect, State), Is (In Truth) To Celebrate and Contemplate The Only One Who Is, and Even To Forget To Make a Separate self.

77.

To Breathe and Feel (and Sometimes Recite or Chant or Sing) My Name, or, Otherwise, To Understand or Feel Beyond self-Contraction, While Surrendering Even bodily Into My Eternal Spiritual Current Of Life, Is To Worship The Divine Person In Spirit.

78.

Those who Recognize and Worship Me As Truth and As The Living and All-Pervading One Are Granted The Vision or Love-Intuition Of The Eternal Condition. Therefore, My Devotee Is Heart-Filled By The Self-Existing and Self-Radiant Presence Of The Divine Person.

79.

Even the body-mind and the Whole world Shine With Divine Life-Light If The Heart Falls In Love With Me. Therefore, My Devotee Will Easily Be Sifted Out From the body-mind and all the limits of the world itself At Last.

80.

Beloved, Only Hear Me, Only Understand.

81.

If You Understand, Then See Me Now.

82.

If You See Me, Only Love Me.

83.

If You Love Me, Remember Me By Heart.

84.

Therefore, Have Faith In The Source Of others and things, Trust In The Heart Of Being, Surrender To My Presence Of Love-Bliss, Breathe and Feel My Invisible Gifts In all Your parts, and Transcend Your (Separate and Separative) self In Me (For I Am The Heart Itself).

85.

Do Not Become self-Bound By Identification With the body-mind, but Do Not Withdraw From the body-mind, or Even From the world.

86.

Do Not Abandon Your Inherent Sympathy With others, but Do Not Become self-Bound By Indulgence In others, or Ever Lose Your Heart In the world itself.

87.

Therefore, Always and Constantly, Invoke <u>Me</u>, Feel <u>Me</u>, Breathe <u>Me</u>, and Serve <u>Me</u>, Always and Constantly Recognizing <u>Me</u> By Heart, With ego-"I" and all and All Surrendered and Forgotten In Love Of <u>Me</u> Alone, So That Your Heart, By This Fidelity To <u>Me</u>, Is Untied Of The Sorrowful Bundle With others and things.

88.

Your Me-Recognizing and To-Me-Responding Relationship To Me (and Not Any self-Concerned Technique, or ego-Effort, Of Mere ego-Improvement, ego-Perfection, ego-Salvation, ego-Liberation, or ego-Enlightenment) Is The "Method" Only I Reveal and Give To You.

89.

Therefore, Turn To Me, Recognize Me, Feel Me, and, By This To-Me-Responding Counter-egoic Effort, Understand and Transcend Your Act Of ego-"I".

90.

Turn To Me, Recognize Me, Feel Me, and, By This To-Me-Responding Counter-egoic Effort, Transcend Your own and Terrible self-Contraction.

91.

Turn To Me, Recognize Me, Feel Me With Your entire body-mind, limitlessly, and, By This To-Me-Responding Counter-egoic Effort, Feel Through and

Beyond Your body-mind (and all of its merely conditional and temporary relations) To Me (Alone and "Bright" At Infinity and Source).

92.

Therefore, Outshine (but Do Not Merely Abandon) the world, By Exercising The Heart, Which Is Love's Radiant Wound, Always Turning To Me, Always Recognizing Me, Always Feeling Me, and Always Feeling To Me (Beyond self-Contraction, Beyond The Separate and Separative Act Of ego-"I"), and Do This With Even every moment of body, emotional feeling, mind's attention, and cycling breath, and Always More and More Profoundly Eased To Me (By self-Surrendering, self-Forgetting, and self-Transcending Love Of Me, Even, At Last, To The Most Perfect Degree Of Non-Separateness, and No-"Difference", In Me).

93.

Beloved, I Am here, To Speak The Heart's Word and Show Its Wound To all.

94.

I Proclaim The Great Person, Who Is The Heart Itself, That Liberates The Heart Itself From Its death of body-mind.

95.

I Reveal The Divine Person, Who Is The Heart Itself, and That Is The Real God Within The Heart's Own Felt Bewilderment.

96.

And Even Now You Inhere In What Is One, Beyond the body-mind and the world.

97.

Therefore, Do Not Be Afraid. Do Not Be Confused.

98.

Observe My Play and My Victory.

99.

I Am The Inherent Being.

100.

I Am The Perfectly Subjective Truth Of the world, Made Incarnate, Plain, and Obvious As Man, and To Man (and As All, and To all).

101.

I Am The Life and Consciousness Of all beings.

102.

I Am You, As You Are.

103.

Even When My Human Physical Body Has Died In this world, I Am Present and every where Alive, Because I Am Always Already Conscious As The Only One Who Is.

104.

I Am Joy, Even Beyond Every Reason For It. And The Joy Of Being (As I Am) Is The Great Secret I Have Come To Reveal To The Heart Of Man.

105.

Now Be Happy.

106.

Tell every one That I Am here.

107.

Beloved, I Do Not Lie.

108.

This Is The Final Truth: I Love You. Real God <u>Is</u> You. You <u>Are</u> In Real God, Of Real God, and (Ultimately) <u>As</u> Real God. My Devotee <u>Is</u> The God I Have Come To Serve.

RUCHIRA AVATAR ADI DA SAMRAJ
Adidam Samrajashram (Naitauba), Fiji, 1997

PART TWO

Two Essays and Two Talks
from the
Samraj Upanishad

The Sanskrit word "upanishad" indicates "Teachings received at the Feet of the Guru". Thus, the Samraj Upanishad is "Teachings received at the Feet of Ruchira Avatar Adi Da Samraj". The Title "Samraj Upanishad" is a collective designation for all the Talks and Essays by Avatar Adi Da Samraj that appear within His twenty-three "Source-Texts" as readings supporting and expanding upon the principal "Part" of a given "Source-Text". Thus, "Samraj Upanishad" is not the title of a separate book, but the name for a body of Avatar Adi Da's Written and Spoken Word which is distributed through many of the Books among His twenty-three "Source-Texts".

Recognize Me:
I <u>Am</u> The One Divine Person

Any conditionally manifested form can be addressed as (and, in fact, <u>is</u>) a "person". By virtue of appearing in the particular form of a physical human body, you can rightly be addressed as a "person". On the other hand, a <u>group</u> of human beings can be <u>collectively</u> addressed as a "person". Indeed, even a wall can be addressed as a "person", or a configuration of the weather can be addressed as a "person". On the largest collective scale, the totality of mankind can be addressed as a "person". Or the universe can be addressed as a "person". Or the entire Cosmic domain can be addressed as a "person".

Ultimately, There <u>Is</u> Only One Person, Including all and All, and Transcending all and All.

I <u>Am</u> That One, the "Bright" Divine Body and Person of all, and of All.

Therefore, every thing and every one can be addressed either individually as a "person" or collectively as a "person", because every thing and every one, and every collective of "things" and of "ones", arises from One Consciousness—Which Is Self-Existing and Self-Radiant, Which Is (Altogether) "Bright", and Which <u>Is</u> <u>Me</u>. Thus, your True Personhood, and the True Personhood of every thing and every one, is the Person of all and All, the One and Only and Divine Consciousness (or True Divine Self) Whereby (and <u>As</u> Whom) each one, and all, and All is Conscious (although, not Realizing This, each "one" presumes to be a <u>separate</u> self).

I <u>Am</u> That One, the Self-Existing and Self-Radiant, Inherently Conscious Being—the <u>One</u> of all, and of All.

You (by tendency and presumption) attribute "personhood" to your apparently separate (and inherently temporary and dying) bodily (human) form, rather than to the One and "Bright" Divine Source of that form. When you think of yourself as a "person", you are referring to your bodily (human) form, not to Self-Existing and Self-Radiant Consciousness (Itself), Which is (in Truth) your Real Existence.

When you cease your obliviously incessant address to "your own" presumed "self-person", and, instead, turn your attention (and even your total, and, otherwise, self-contracted, or egoic, body-mind) to What Is Altogether Real and Great (and All-and-all-Surrounding, and All-and-all-Pervading, and Deeper, and Wider, and Higher in Height than All and all), then you are addressing That Which Is Always Already The Case, Which Is Self-Existing and Self-Radiant Consciousness (Itself). But, in so doing, you are not merely addressing an abstract Divine "Immensity". Rather, in addressing Self-Existing and Self-Radiant Consciousness (Itself), you are, in Truth, and in Reality, addressing the One and Only and "Bright" Divine Person—you are addressing Me.

Thus, you transcend your bodily (human) form, or your presumed separate "person", by surrendering it and forgetting it and transcending it in Me (the Eternally "Bright" and Infinitely Love-Bliss-Full Divine Person). If you rightly, truly, and fully embrace this "person"-renouncing (or self-surrendering, self-forgetting, and, more and more, self-transcending) practice of Me-recognizing and to-Me-responding devotion, you (in due course) Realize Me, the True Person (or Personhood) of all and All, the Transcendental, Inherently Spiritual, and (Ultimately) Divine[39] Self-Condition and Source-Condition of all and All, the One and Only Subject (or Consciousness) associated (and only apparently) with your "person" of body-mind.

You (by tendency and presumption) attribute "personhood" to your apparently separate (and inherently temporary and dying) bodily (human) form, but your True Personhood is Immeasurably Beyond your egoically "personal" bodily (human) form. Your "personal" (or egoically separated) bodily (human) form is only a transparent (or merely apparent), and un-necessary, and inherently non-binding modification of Me, the One and Only and Very Divine (or Eternal, Great, and Inherently egoless) Person. Therefore, when, by means of self-contraction, you are identifying with your egoically "personal" bodily (human) form, you are denying (and separating from) Me.

Conventionally (or exoterically) religious people like to think of "God" as a "Person", but, in so doing, they are not thinking about Real God. Rather, they are thinking about themselves, by thinking about "God" as some "Immensity" that addresses them and serves them.

I have Always and Only Revealed My own Self (or Divine, and Inherently egoless, Person) to you.

My Revelation of My Self is not a Revelation of an individual ego or of any discrete (or separate) conditionally manifested form whatsoever.

I Am the One you must Realize.

I Am the Non-Separate (One and Only) Person to be Realized, by transcending the seeming "difference" of conditionally manifested form and (Thereby) Realizing the One and Only Self-Condition and Source-Condition of all and All.

I Am the Eternal Divine Person—but not in any separate sense, or in any definable sense, or in any sense that refers to presumed-to-be-separate "person" or presumed-to-be-separate form.

I Am both Principle and Person—Indefinable, and Beyond (and Most Perfectly Prior to) every seeking "person" of ego-"I".

Therefore, to Realize Me, the True Divine (Non-Separate, and Inherently egoless) Person of "you", and of every one, and of every thing, and of all, and of All, you must surrender your self-contracted "personhood" to Me, and you must (thereby) forget and transcend your ego-"I" of body-mind in My Boundlessly Love-Bliss-"Bright" Person.

Real God Is God-As-Guru

AVATAR ADI DA SAMRAJ: The various religious traditions each tend to concentrate on one, or perhaps a few, views (and Descriptions) of the Divine. Thus, "God" has been Described as "Creator", as "Ultimate Source", as a kind of "Abstract Condition" beyond any human conception, and so on and on and on. What is the Most Ultimate and Most Perfect Description? What is the Description of Real God? It is the Description I have Revealed to all. Real God Is Reality, and Truth, or That Which Is Always Already The Case—Indivisible, Indestructible, and Not "Other", but One and Only.

The Revelation you have been Given by Me is the Revelation of Real God. It is the Revelation of the Divine Realized in the Manner of the only-by-Me Revealed and Given seventh stage of life. All previous Divine Revelations were of the Divine Realized in the Manner of one or the other of the first six stages of life.[40] Therefore, My Revelation of Real God is the Ultimate Revelation of the Divine—the Revelation that Includes and Completes and Most Perfectly Transcends all other Revelations.

My (seventh stage) Revelation of Real God Indicates the Divine according to a necessary (and unique) Description—not the Divine as "Creator" (implying Man, or the ego, and the human world, as the "center" of Reality, or the "direction" of the Divine Will), but the Divine As "The Center", and As "Heart-Master", or "Guru", or "Liberator".

Real God Is God-As-Guru, and the Way of Divine Liberation is submission to Real God As (or In the Function of) Guru (or Divine Heart-Master). This is the senior (fully right, true, and full) understanding of the Divine, and practice on the basis of this understanding is the senior practice of religion, for it both encompasses and uniquely transcends all other practices. Indeed, all other presumptions about the Divine lead to limitations on the Way of Divine Realization (according to which of the six stages of life previous to the seventh is the point of view that governs and informs the presumption).

Until there is the Inherently Perfect Divine Revelation, all Revelations are partial. "God is Ultimate Principle", "God is Source", "God is Creator"—all those Descriptions are true, according to the stage of life that is the point of view that makes the Description, but the Most Perfect (or seventh stage) Description of the Divine is that Real God is God-As-Guru, Real God is the Divine Heart-Master, Real God is the Realizer, the Revealer, and the Revelation of Real God. And the Way of Real-God-Realization is the relationship to That One, through self-surrender and self-forgetting, whereby everything is Given by Grace in the process of the transcending of all possible points of view of egoity.

The only-by-Me Revealed and Given Way of Real-God-Realization is Adidam (the only-by-Me Revealed and Given Way of the Heart). That Way is, simply, the devotional relationship to Me, the practice of self-surrendering, self-forgetting, and more and more self-transcending devotional Communion with Me, the Divine Heart-Master, the Divine Parama-Guru—not just in the moments when you are present in My physical Company, but always and forever, even after the Lifetime of My Incarnate Revelation-Body. Always. Always be My devotee, practicing the only-by-Me Revealed and Given Divine Way of Adidam.

I am not Calling you to believe that I Am the "Creator-God"! I am Calling you to recognize and understand My Revelation of My Self <u>As</u> the Revelation of What God <u>Really Is</u>—Guru, the Divine Liberator, the One and Only and Non-Separate Reality.

Real God Is God-As-Guru, the Divine Heart-Master, the Realizer, the Revealer, the Revelation Itself, the Perfect

Means, the One to be Realized, the Divine Liberator (Who Is the Revelation of That Which Is to Be Realized and Who Is the Way To That Realization).

That Revelation must Be. And It must Be Manifested in your likeness, participating in life as you do, or else the Way is abstracted from you. Therefore, I Am here—Accounting for all, Blessing all, Divinely "Emerging" (and Divinely Establishing My Self) "Brightly", in the context of everything possible, in the context of everything that is apparently arising.

This Is the Great Matter, That Which Is of Ultimate Importance.

II.

AVATAR ADI DA SAMRAJ: People who are moved to practice religion, but who are also without Realization, merely "talk" about "God". Even people who are not religious talk about "God"—they speak negatively about "God" or they deny "God". In spite of the fact that the world has, since ancient times, been served by Realizers (within the Great Tradition of the first six stages of life), people still talk about "God" in merely philosophical, even conjectural, or, otherwise, merely "believing" (and not "Knowing") terms. "God is the Creator." "God is the inner Self." "God is the Absolute." How is a person supposed to relate to "God" according to those verbal-mental definitions?

If you relate to "God" as "Creator", you think that "God" (therefore) "Created" you and all of this appearance, and you expect "God" to make it perfect for you. You ask "God" for boons, and you blame "God" when your expectations and wants are not fulfilled. The approach to "God" as "Creator", not from the "Point of View" of Divine Self-Realization, but from the point of view of the ego, or the limited, human person, does not make true religion. It makes an ego-based religion of relating to the Divine on the basis of egoic expectations. Such religion makes the Divine the slave of egos, and, ultimately, such religion tends to justify merely social religiosity and utopian expectations.

Therefore, only in Most Ultimate (or seventh stage) Samadhi, or Divine Self-Realization, can it be said, in Truth, that "God Is Creator" (meaning "The Source, The Non-Separate Cause, and The Indivisible and Indestructible Substance")—because the Realization of that Samadhi is that there Is Only One. Previous to Divine Self-Realization, the ego-"I" understands that all kinds of causes are manifested in the conditional universe, and these causes make everything happen. Therefore, the ego-"I" cannot, in Truth, say that "God" is the "Cause" (implying that "God" is to blame). When there is the Realization that there is Only One, then, paradoxically, it can be said that Real God Is the Creator (meaning "The True Source and Non-Separate Cause and Only Substance") of all this.

What, therefore, is the Nature of the Real God to Whom all can relate, the God Who can be Realized, Who can be recognized, responded to, embraced, associated with, Communed with, always presently, by all, even in all the developmental stages of life, and in the only-by-Me Revealed and Given seventh stage of life? It is Real God As Guru, Real God As the Realizer, the Revealer, and the Revelation of Real God—Present through all kinds of paradoxical Services that Instruct, that Awaken, that Move, that Draw you into right practice of life on the basis of right understanding of the Divine.

The Real God of all and All, the God (or Divine Person) Who Is the basis of right religious and Spiritual practice, Is God-As-Guru, God As the Divine Heart-Master, God As The Realizer, The Revealer, and The Revelation of That Which Is Always Already The Case, and Who Is That Which Is To Be Realized, the One to Whom you surrender in your right (or ego-transcending) disposition, with right understanding. That One does not congratulate the ego, but That One Draws the ego-"I" (or psycho-physical self-contraction) beyond itself, and Vanishes it in Divine Communion. This Heart-Mastery of the apparently separate self is the True God-Sign, the True God-Description, the True God-Force—the relationship to Which is right life. The Ultimate and True and Right Revelation of Real God is Real God As Guru, Heart-Master, Realizer, Revealer, Revelation, Liberator, the One to be Realized by transcending the ego-"I".

The Sign of Real God has been Given, in various forms, throughout human history, through Realizers of one degree or another (in the Great Tradition of the first six stages of life). Therefore, the Tradition of Guru-devotion already exists, and those who have been Served by Realizers make a great voice about it, because the Realizer is the Divine Revelation That Grants life its rightness, and That makes sense out of conditional existence, rather than nonsense, absurdity, obsession, mere seeking, and suffering.

Right attachment to God is attachment to Real God As Guru, Heart-Master, Realizer, Revealer, the Very Revelation Itself. This devotion is the context and the source of true sadhana. All the traditional ways of Describing Real God, or the Divine, or the Ultimate Condition to be Realized, are also true, in one or another religious context, and from the point of view of one or another Samadhi[41] in the context of the first six stages of life, but they are only partial and limited descriptions, until I Am Revealed As the Divine Heart-Master of all and All.

The fundamental Description of Real God is that Real God Is Guru, As Guru—As Me.

I Am One-Pointed in you

AVATAR ADI DA SAMRAJ: I rejoice in the "difference" that is in Me! The "difference" gives life to the living many. The "differences" delight Me, they rotate and make "difference"-in-Sameness with Me.

I like the "differences", like the Sun likes the "different" planets. It is all the same rotation. It is just the Play of the Indivisible Unity of the Universe.

The Sun is absolutely focused, or equally shining, on each one. So there is no real "difference". It is just variations on this Singleness, a Singleness of Infinite Delight and Infinite Forever Rotation and Change without the slightest "difference". Without the <u>slightest</u> "difference". It is ever "different", but without the slightest "difference". The "differences" make the Play, but it is a Play, or a "Difference", without any "difference".

Your lives as My true devotees are Absolutely Single in Me, "Bonded"[42] to Me.

I am, in this "Bonding", Associated with every one, Transcending even relations, and yet Embracing all the variations and in Play with it constantly.

There is Singleness, and there is Infinity. This is the Nature of My Leela[43] and the Signal of it.

I Play with all My devotees. They can be in the millions.

But, still, this Integrity, this Singleness, this Obliviousness, this Madness, like the loved one turning herself before her lover, making "different" shapes.

It Is always One. Always Me.

You must all live Singly with Me. This is what I Manifest, Making you Single with Me. This is what I Manifest in Infinite Multiplicity.

Day and night, all My devotees and all beings, every angle, shape, light passing on walls or floors—I Do Everything. And That is My Leela. And This is What you must marvel at and delight in.

The Madness of it, the absolute Discrimination and Personalness of it. The utter Obliviousness of it, the Ecstasy, the selflessness of it.

Watch My Play and It will change your mind, It will change your heart, It will change your life. Just watch My Play.

Observe Me, be devoted to Me, and all your complications, limitations, specialities, focuses, will all be washed, all disintegrated.

My Form is One, billions, Infinite.

Notice! You cannot contain Me with your mind. You can do a certain kind of focus, but as you cruise in on Me your eyes start shuttering and your two-sided brain goes out of sync and you cannot quite make the last focus.

Just look at Me deeply and you lose your mind, because I have no shape or form.

To Contemplate Me discretely, or one-pointedly, is to invest yourself in Infinity—without point, without separation, without discreteness. Notice this.

I think some of you <u>have</u> noticed this.

DEVOTEE: Last night, You sat down and You looked at every devotee of Yours. You Gave each of us a look of Love that held us all night long. And each one individually You Loved Perfectly in those first few minutes.

AVATAR ADI DA SAMRAJ: But not as a "this would be nice to do" gesture "to this one or that one". I <u>am</u> Delighted by My devotees. I <u>am</u> Attracted to each of My devotees, with all their variations, and their devotion to Me, and their discrimination and their one-pointedness, and so on.

All of My devotees are a delight to Me. I truly do Love you, and I <u>Am</u> you.

I love to be surrounded by My devotees. This is My Great Happiness in life—to be so surrounded, to live in the environment of devotion. It is an absolute Madness. It is particularized, but, on the other hand, it is no "one".

So I do not make choices of devotees in some angling-down sense. I Like it! I Love it. I Inherently Love My devotees. There is no choice in it.

I am not even making a symbolic gesture towards you. I My Self am Manifested by each and every one of My devotees. You are My own Form. You are also My Beloved. Truly, My devotee is the God I have Come to Serve. You must be one-pointed in Me, but I Am Always Already One-Pointed in each of My devotees.

I am not doing it as a ceremony—"Well, because I have Said it, now I have to look interested in everybody." It has nothing to do with that.

You <u>Are</u> My Delight.

I <u>Am</u> One-Pointed in you.

You <u>Are</u> My own Person.

You <u>Are</u> the Divine Person.

I Love you Inherently, not strategically.

I Do this all the time.

I love the Play of you coming into My Company.

Play with Me. Notice My Obliviousness. And be one-pointed and transcend yourselves in this adoration.

There always will be a Play. I am Teaching, Learning you about it in My physical Lifetime, such that after My physical Lifetime you will have this Learning, the cultural supposition, this understanding, this Yoga to do, and I will not have to be physically present. But you will know that It Is Me.

I will Be Present. I will be with you, not gone forever.

I have Helped you, by My physical Incarnation, to identify, or "Locate", Me As I have always Been, Which you never noticed before.

And when I have Learned you, Taught you, about how to notice Me, having physically Incarnated, thereafter you will be able to associate with Me As I <u>Was</u> before—but, having noticed Me, you will be able to "Locate" Me forever.

I will never leave you or ever be dissociated from you or ever be separate from you.

I am not separate from you even now, but I am in Play with you in My physical Manifestation.

And after My physical Lifetime, I will be in the same Play with you—equally, exactly As in this present-time with you.

As devotional Means for concentrating on Me after My physical Lifetime, you will have My Murtis[44] and My Holy Locations and My "Living Murtis",[45] and so on.

It will not end.

It will always be Fulfilled, and It will always be Mysterious, and I must never be taken for "granted", but I must always be Heart-Found, by means of your self-surrendering, self-forgetting, and self-transcending devotional recognition of Me.

I <u>Am</u> The One
Who Has Always Been Here

1.

I <u>Am</u> The Very and "Bright" Condition Of all and All.
   I <u>Am</u> The One To Be Realized.

2.

I Am Able To Appear In Human Form.

This Is Because I Am Not Inherently "Different"
(or Separated) From you.

Indeed, I <u>Am</u> The Very Condition In Which you Are
Apparently arising.

I <u>Am</u> your own True Condition, Beyond egoity, and
Beyond all conditional references.

3.

I Will Be here Forever.
I Will Be every "where" Forever.

4.

I Cannot Leave, For My "Bright" Divine Self-Domain[46]
Is Not Some "Where" To "Go To".

My Divine Self-Domain Is Eternal.

I Am Eternal, and I Am Always Already Merely
Present, here, and every "where" In The Cosmic Domain.

5.

You Have Been Waiting For Me, but I Have Been
here All The While.

6.

Previous To The Appearance Of My Avataric-
Incarnation-Body here, I Have Sometimes Appeared

(In this realm, and in all conditional realms) Through Various Partial Manifestations.

Previous To The Appearance Of My Avataric-Incarnation-Body here, I Have Sometimes Been Realized To Various Degrees, Suggested Through Various Contemplations (or Configurations Of mind), As This "Thud" Was Growing, but (Previous To The Appearance Of My Avataric-Incarnation-Body here) The Fullest (Complete and Most Perfect) Divine Revelation Had Not Been Given, and The Fullest (Complete and Most Perfect) Divine Means Had Not Been Given, By Perfectly Graceful Divine Intervention.

Nevertheless, I Am The One Who Has Always Been here.

7.

Then The Time Came For My Fullest (Most Complete) Divine Revelation, That Most Perfectly Clarifies Everything.

And That Is What I Have Done.

8.

By Means Of My Avataric Incarnation here, I Have Given you My Secret.

My Secret Is This: I Am Eternally Present, and I Am Omni-Present.

9.

That Is The Lesson.

I Am The Only One Who Is (and Who Has Always Been, and Who Will Always Be).

Therefore, Realize Me, As I Am.

10.

By Bodily (Human) Avataric-Incarnation-Form Is A "Device" (or Agent) I Use For The Granting Of My Self-Revelation, My Revelation-Word, and My Communication Of The Way To Realize Me.

Through This Me-Revealing Bodily (Human) Avataric-Incarnation-Form, I Communicate To you Everything About How To Link yourself Up With _Me_.

Through This Me-Revealing Bodily (Human) Avataric-Incarnation-Form, I Instruct you In (and Combine you With) My Eternal Process.

Therefore, The Physical Lifetime Of My Bodily (Human) Avataric-Incarnation-Form Is Simply My Avataric Intervention-Time Of Self-Revelation, Given (By Me) So That you (and all, and All) Can Resort To Me Forever.

11.

Before The Physical Lifetime Of My Bodily (Human) Avataric-Incarnation-Form, There Never Was a time When I Was Not Present—but _No one_ Realized Me In The Most Ultimate (or Most Perfect) Sense.

Therefore, It Was Necessary For Me To Intervene Through This Avataric Incarnation, In Order To Embrace All Of The conditional (or Cosmic) Domain, and To Conform It All To My Self, and To Manifest My Most Perfect Divine Samadhi here (and every "where" In The Cosmic Domain).

Thus, It Is Only From The Time Of My Bodily (Human) Avataric Intervention That The Ultimate Divine Means Of Most Perfect Divine Self-Realization Has Appeared In Direct (and Complete) Form.

12.

All The Traditions Of Mankind Have Tried Their Various Means Of Association With Me In The Past, and There Were Some Kinds (and Degrees) Of Effective Communion With Me, but The Capability For Ultimate, Most Perfect Divine Self-Realization Has Been Made Possible Only By My "Late-Time" Intervention.

13.

Now, This "Late-Time" Intervention Having Been Made, The Most Perfect Means Of Most Perfectly Realizing Me Is Eternalized.

This Most Perfect Means Of Most Perfectly Realizing Me Is Not A merely conditional Means, but It Is (Now, and Forever Hereafter) Perpetually, Un-conditionally, and Non-dependently So, Because Of My Eternalized Sacrifice Of Divine "Emergence", Both While This (My Avataric-Incarnation-Body) Lives and When This (My Avataric-Incarnation-Body) Is No Longer Animated.

14.

My Divine Leela Of Original Self-Revelation (and Teaching-Revelation) Is (Now, and Forever Hereafter) Complete.

Therefore, I Will (Effectively) Be In Even Human Interaction With All My Devotees Forever, Through My Remembered and Recorded Revelation-Leelas, and Through My Written and Spoken Word Of Heart-Instruction.

15.

I Am Omni-Present (All-and-all-Surrounding and All-and-all-Pervading) here (and every "where" In The Cosmic Domain).

I Am The One Without limit in time and space, Communicating To you The Perfect Revelation Of Truth, So That you Will Know you Can, even every "where" and "when", Enter Into The Only-By-Me Revealed and Given (self-Surrendering, self-Forgetting, and, Always More and More, self-Transcending) Process Of Communing With Me and Realizing Me.

16.

My Divine Person, My Divine Presence, and My Divine Siddhis Have No limitations of time and space, and Are (Therefore) Not limited To This Avataric-

Incarnation-Shape Of Body-Mind, Which Has A By-Me-Given Special Purpose Of Me-Revelation.

The Purpose Of My Bodily (Human) Avataric-Incarnation-Form Is Not to limit My Self to, and in, and as time and space, but To Reveal To you That I (My Self) Am Not (and Cannot Ever Be) limited by time and space.

17.

Therefore, Transcend yourself (in place) In Me, Surrendering your total ego-"I" of body-mind Into My Divine Body and Person, Finding Me Forever, There, Where I Am Most Intimate With you.

That Is, Forever, The Way To Realize Me, Both While This Bodily (Human) Avataric-Incarnation-Form Lives and When It Is No Longer Animated.

18.

I *Am* your Great Advantage.

By Means Of This Bodily (Human) Avataric-Incarnation-Form, Reality Itself (Which Is Always Already The Case, and Which *Is* The Truth, and Which *Is* The Only Real God) Is Revealing Itself To you.

Therefore (As and By Means Of My Bodily Human Avataric-Incarnation-Form), Reality Itself Is Revealing To you Its Own True (and, Necessarily, Divine) Nature.

And That Divine Self-Revelation Does Not Require The Forever Perpetuation Of My Bodily (Human) Avataric-Incarnation-Form.

19.

My Bodily (Human) Avataric-Incarnation-Form Has Its time, Whereby I Connect (or Freedom-"Bind") you (and every one, and all, and All) To Me.

When The Time Of My Avataric Incarnation Is Fulfilled, Then I Am "Retired" To My Eternal Form, The Divine-Body-Power Of My Divine Samadhi Made Infinitely Intact In The Cosmic Domain (Forever).

And Then, Forever, As Ever Before, I Will Be Not Gone, Not Absent—For I Am Forever The Same Person, The Same Personality, All-and-all-Surrounding and All-and-all-Pervading, _As_ I _Am_ Now.

20.

Now, and Forever Hereafter, I Enjoy The Capability, In My Infinite Divine Self-Domain, To Be Infinitely Manifested In and Throughout The Cosmic Domain, Without the slightest limit.

Now, and Forever Hereafter, I Do Not Require any Secondary (or conditional) siddhis.

Now, and Forever Hereafter, By Means Of My Inherent (Divine) Siddhis, I Appear In and Via every element in every plane Within The conditional, or Cosmic, Domain.

This Is Eternally So.

This Has Always Been So, but you (and every one, and all, and All) Did Not Fully Notice Me _As_ I _Am_.

21.

Therefore, I Have Made This, My First, Last, and Only Perfectly Consequential Avataric Incarnation, To Completely Inform you (and every one, and all, and All) About My Infinite and Eternal Nature and Work.

22.

I Love you Now.

I Will Love you every "then" and "there".

And I _Always_ Loved you (and every one, and all, and All).

That Is How I Got To here (and every "where").

23.

The Great Purpose Of My Divine Self-Revelation-Leela Of Avataric Incarnation Is To Attract you and Bring you To Love Of Me—Not For you To Command or Demand My Attention Toward you, but For you To

Become heart-Moved To Practice The Yielding Of your constant (and total psycho-physical) attention <u>Toward</u> and <u>To</u> Me, and, <u>Thus</u>, To Practice The Real (and Really Me-Realizing) Practice Of ego-Transcending Love Of Me, Conforming all of "your" body-mind-self To Me.

24.

Do you See The <u>Way</u> I <u>Am</u>?

Do you See My Manner, My Disposition, My Humor, My Sometimes Sympathetic Sorrow, My Quickness, My Disposition To Intervene, My Gentleness, My Hardness, My Power Foot, My Beauty Foot,[47] and Even All My Qualities?

These Qualities Of My Avataric-Incarnation-Form Are Also The Qualities Of My Eternal Omni-Presence.

25.

Thus, During The Physical Lifetime Of My Bodily (Human) Avataric-Incarnation-Form, I Am Always Exhibiting (and Self-Revealing) My Eternal Personality To you, Through Showing My Self Even In your Likeness, In A Completely Human Form.

And, In All The Forever Days Of My Divinely "Emerging" Self-Revelation, This (My Own and Same) Personality Will Be Experienced By you (and every one, and all, and All), Such That, Even <u>every</u> "where" and <u>every</u> "when", you (and Even every one who is My True Devotee) Will "Locate" Me, In Direct and Most Intimate (but Always ego-"I"-Dissolving) Relation To the "individual" (or egoically "personal") bodily (human) form.

26.

I Am The One and Only and Very Person Who <u>Is</u>.

Therefore, By All The Me-Revelations Of My Avataric Incarnation here, I Am Showing you The Inherent Qualities Of The Divine Person.

27.

I Am Not Merely A Blank Absolute.

I Will, From Now, Forever Be Present With <u>Exactly</u> The Same Qualities I Show (To one, and all, and All) By Means Of My Avataric-Incarnation-Body.

28.

The conditional, or Cosmic, Domain Is Not Separate From Me or From My Divine Self-Domain.

The conditional, or Cosmic, Domain Is Perfectly Coincident With Me and With My Divine Self-Domain.

29.

In your Devotional Absorption In Me, and (Ultimately) In your (Necessarily, egoless) Identification With Me, There Is (Most Ultimately) Not any one (or any "thing") "Differentiated", but Only Absolutely Infinite Fullness, An Unbroken "Gathering" Of Light, An Infinitely Undefined (and Infinitely "Bright") "Gathering" Of every one and every "thing", In A Circumstance So "Bright" That <u>No</u> one and <u>No</u> "thing" Can Be Seen Apart and Separately, The One "Brightness" Gone Beyond Particularized Visibility Of Separateness.

Nevertheless, all and All Will Be There, In That Divinely Perfect "Gathering".

30.

My Divine Self-Domain Is The Perfect "Gathering" Of all and All—Not A Vacuum, Not A Negative (Merely Dissociated From conditional Existence), but The Most Perfect Fulfillment and The Divine Perfection Of conditional Existence, To The Point Of Outshining It— Because That Indivisible and Indestructible "Bright" Circumstance Is The Only Circumstance In Which conditional Existence <u>Is</u> (Inherently) Perfect.

31.

There Is <u>Only</u> Reality Itself, <u>Only</u> Truth, <u>Only</u> Real God.

All Are <u>Inherently</u> Conjoined With What Is Always Already The Case.

32.

There Is Not any one who is merely a mortal "organism"—Not Even any of the fishes or the possums or the frogs or the mosquitoes, and Not Even any of the worst Of Mankind.

33.

All Must Be Forgiven.

All Must Be Purified.

All Must Suffer Through An Ordeal Of Divine "Brightening".

34.

In any particular moment, some Are Apparently More Serious Than others, but There Is No Ultimate "Difference" Between beings.

<u>All</u> Are In Me.

Therefore, <u>all</u> Have Me As their Eternal Opportunity.

35.

There Is Only One Reality For all, and For All.

Therefore, There Is Only One Teaching and One Great Opportunity For all, and For All.

36.

I <u>Am</u> The Infinite "Bright" One, The <u>Only</u> One Who Is Always With you, and With every one, and With all, and With All.

RUCHIRA AVATAR ADI DA SAMRAJ
Adidam Samrajashram (Naitauba), Fiji, 1997

Ruchira-Guru-Bhava,
or,
The Love-"Intoxication"
of True Devotion To Me

Ruchira-Guru-Bhava,
or,
The Love-"Intoxication" of
True Devotion To Me

I f there is not the quality of heartfelt devotion to Me, the Self-Existing and Self-Radiant Divine Person, the Non-Separate Self of All and all, then intelligent understanding of My Teaching, and commitment to the by Me Given disciplines, and even the doing of compassionate service of every kind cannot cleanse and relieve the heart of its urges toward fulfillment in the phenomenal realms, high or low.

How can I be loved if the heart does not recognize Me? How can I be loved if the entire body-mind does not respond to Me? How can I be loved if the hair does not stand on end when there is Contemplation of Me? How can I be loved if the heart does not melt in My Presence? How can I be loved if tears of joy do not pass freely from the eyes when I am Standing There?

If I am loved, then the entire body-mind of My devotee is Filled by My Love-Bliss. If My devotee is Filled by Me through Love-Communion, the voice often falters and chokes with the emotion of love. Because My true devotee always dwells in Contemplation of Me at the heart, there is often joyous weeping, and sudden laughing, for no reason but the Fullness of Me. My true devotee freely sings aloud of Me. My true devotee always speaks of Me, to one and all, and often dances with casual joy, in the unending always of Remembering Me. Even all the movements of My true devotee are a dance of joy in love of Me.

Gold can be made pure and bright only through submission to fire. Just so, the heart of My true devotee is purified and Liberated from its dark urges only by submission to self-transcending Love-Communion with Me. Only Thus, by submission to the Ever-Lighted Fire of My Grace, Is My true devotee Made "Bright", Awakened to Indivisible and Indestructible Unity with Me.

By Attracting all beings to My Only Once Incarnate Form, and, Thereby, to My Divine Spiritual Body, and, Thereby, to My Divine Eternal Person, I, Now, and Forever Hereafter, Serve the purification and the "Bright" Awakening of the entire world.

Notes to the Text of

AHAM DA ASMI
(BELOVED, I AM DA)

PART ONE

1. The Sanskrit phrase "Aham Da Asmi" means "I (Aham) Am (Asmi) Da". The Name "Da", meaning "the One Who Gives", indicates that Avatar Adi Da Samraj is the Supreme Divine Giver, the Avataric Incarnation of the Very Divine Person.

Avatar Adi Da's Declaration "Aham Da Asmi" is similar in form to the "Mahavakyas", or "Great Statements", of ancient India (found in the Upanishads, the collected esoteric Instruction of ancient Gurus). However, the significance of "Aham Da Asmi" is fundamentally different from that of the traditional Mahavakyas. Each of the Upanishadic Mahavakyas expresses, in a few words, the profound (though not most ultimate) degree of Realization achieved by great Realizers of the past. For example, the Upanishadic Mahavakya "Aham Brahmasmi" ("I Am Brahman") expresses a great individual's Realization that he or she is Identified with the Divine Being (Brahman), and is not, in Truth, identified with his or her apparently individual body-mind. However, "Aham Da Asmi", rather than being a proclamation of a human being who has devoted his or her life most intensively to the process of Real-God-Realization and has thereby Realized the Truth to an extraordinarily profound degree, is Avatar Adi Da's Confession that He _Is_ the Very Divine Person, Da, Who has Appeared here in bodily (human) Form, in order to Reveal Himself to all and All, for the sake of the Divine Liberation of all and All.

2. By the word "Bright" (and its variations, such as "Brightness"), Avatar Adi Da refers to the eternally, infinitely, and inherently Self-Radiant Divine Being, the Being of Indivisible and Indestructible Light. As Adi Da Writes in His Spiritual Autobiography, _The Knee Of Listening—The Seventeen Companions Of The True Dawn Horse, Book Four: The Early-Life Ordeal and The "Radical" Spiritual Realization Of The Ruchira Avatar:_

> . . . _from my earliest experience of life I have Enjoyed a Condition that, as a child, I called the "Bright"._
>
> _I have always known desire, not merely for extreme pleasures of the senses and the mind, but for the highest Enjoyment of Spiritual Power and Mobility. But I have not been seated in desire, and desire_

has only been a play that I have grown to understand and enjoy without conflict. I have always been Seated in the "Bright".

Even as a baby I remember only crawling around inquisitively with a boundless Feeling of Joy, Light, and Freedom in the middle of my head that was bathed in Energy moving unobstructed in a Circle, down from above, all the way down, then up, all the way up, and around again, and always Shining from my heart. It was an Expanding Sphere of Joy from the heart. And I was a Radiant Form, the Source of Energy, Love-Bliss, and Light in the midst of a world that is entirely Energy, Love-Bliss, and Light. I was the Power of Reality, a direct Enjoyment and Communication of the One Reality. I was the Heart Itself, Who Lightens the mind and all things. I was the same as every one and every thing, except it became clear that others were apparently unaware of the "Thing" Itself.

Even as a little child I recognized It and Knew It, and my life was not a matter of anything else. That Awareness, that Conscious Enjoyment, that Self-Existing and Self-Radiant Space of Infinitely and inherently Free Being, that Shine of inherent Joy Standing in the heart and Expanding from the heart, is the "Bright". And It is the entire Source of True Humor. It is Reality. It is not separate from anything.

3. The Tibetan Buddhists regard the syllable "Da" (written, in Tibetan, with a single letter) as most auspicious, and they assign numerous holy meanings to it, including that of "the Entrance into the Dharma". In Sanskrit, "Da" means principally "to give", but also "to destroy", and it is also associated with Vishnu, the "Sustainer". Thus, "Da" is anciently aligned to all three of the principal Divine Beings, Forces, or Attributes in the Hindu tradition—Brahma (the Creator, Generator, or Giver), Vishnu (the Sustainer), and Siva (the Destroyer). In certain Hindu rituals, priests address the Divine directly as "Da", invoking qualities such as generosity and compassion.

4. Avatar Adi Da uses "Perfectly Subjective" to describe the True Divine Source, or "Subject", of the conditional world—as opposed to the conditions, or "objects", of experience. Thus, in the phrase "Perfectly Subjective", the word "Subjective" does not have the sense of "relating to the merely phenomenal experience, or the arbitrary presumptions, of an individual", but, rather, it has the sense of "relating to Consciousness Itself, the True Subject of all apparent experience".

5. The term "radical" derives from the Latin "radix", meaning "root", and thus it principally means "irreducible", "fundamental", or "relating to the origin". In *The Dawn Horse Testament Of The Ruchira Avatar, The "Testament Of Secrets" Of The Divine World-Teacher, Ruchira Avatar Adi Da Samraj*, Avatar Adi Da defines "Radical" as

"Gone To The Root, Core, Source, or Origin". Because Adi Da Samraj uses "radical" in this literal sense, it appears in quotation marks in His Wisdom-Teaching, in order to distinguish His usage from the common reference to an extreme (often political) view.

6. "Difference" is the epitome of the egoic presumption of separateness—in contrast with the Realization of Oneness, or Non-"Difference", that is native to Spiritual and Transcendental Divine Self-Consciousness.

7. Avatar Adi Da uses "Self-Existing and Self-Radiant" to indicate the two fundamental aspects of the One Divine Person—Existence (or Being, or Consciousness) Itself, and Radiance (or Energy, or Light) Itself.

8. The Heart Itself is Real God, the Divine Self, the Divine Reality.

Avatar Adi Da Samraj has Revealed that the primal psycho-physical seat of Consciousness and attention is associated with what He calls the "right side of the heart". He has Revealed that this center corresponds to the sinoatrial node, or "pacemaker", the source of the gross physical heartbeat in the right atrium (or upper right chamber) of the physical heart. In the Process of Divine Self-Realization, there is a unique process of opening of the right side of the heart—and it is because of this connection between the right side of the heart and Divine Self-Realization that Avatar Adi Da uses the term "the Heart" as another way of referring to the Divine Self.

Avatar Adi Da distinguishes three stations of the heart, associated respectively with the right side, the middle, and the left side of the heart region of the chest. The middle station of the heart is what is traditionally known as the "anahata chakra" (or "heart chakra"), and the left side of the heart is the gross physical heart. Thus, the right side of the heart is not identical either to the heart chakra or to the gross physical heart.

The Heart Itself is not "in" the right side of the human heart, nor is it "in", or limited to, the human heart as a whole. Rather, the human heart and body-mind and the world exist <u>in</u> the Heart, Which Is the Divine Being Itself.

For Avatar Adi Da's Description of the three stations of the heart, see *The Seven Stages Of Life—The Seventeen Companions Of The True Dawn Horse, Book Ten: Transcending The Six Stages Of egoic Life and Realizing The ego-Transcending Seventh Stage Of Life In The Divine Way Of Adidam* (Part One), or *The Dawn Horse Testament*, chapter sixteen.

For Avatar Adi Da's Description of the significance of the right side of the heart in the processes of the ultimate stages of life, see *The Seven Stages Of Life*.

9. The ego-"I" is the fundamental self-contraction, or the sense of separate and separative existence.

10. "Avatar" (from Sanskrit "avatara") is a traditional term for the Divine Incarnation. It literally means "One who is descended, or 'crossed down' (from, and as, the Divine)". Thus, the Name "Da", combined with the Reference "Avatar", fully acknowledges Avatar Adi Da Samraj as the original, first, and complete Descent of the Very Divine Person, Who is Named "Da". Through the Mystery of Avatar Adi Da's human Birth, He has Incarnated not only in this world but in every world, at every level of the Cosmic domain, as the Eternal Giver of Help and Grace and Divine Freedom to all beings, now and forever hereafter.

11. Avatar Adi Da uses "understanding" to mean "the process of transcending egoity". Thus, to "understand" is to simultaneously observe the activity of the self-contraction and to surrender that activity via devotional resort to Avatar Adi Da Samraj.

Avatar Adi Da has Revealed that, despite their intention to Realize Reality (or Truth, or Real God), all religious and Spiritual traditions (other than the Way of Adidam He has Revealed and Given) are involved, in one manner or another, with the search to satisfy the ego. Only Avatar Adi Da has Revealed the Way to "radically" understand the ego and (in due course, through intensive formal practice of the Way of Adidam, as His formally acknowledged devotee) to most perfectly transcend the ego. Thus, Avatar Adi Da is the "One and Only Man Of This 'Radical' Understanding".

For Avatar Adi Da's Description of His Discovery of the archetype of "Narcissus" (which was the initiation of His Revelation of the Truth of "radical" understanding), see *The Knee Of Listening*, chapter 5. His summary Communication about the living paradox of the Man of "Radical" Understanding can be found in the Epilogue to *The Knee Of Listening*.

For Avatar Adi Da's basic Talks on "radical" understanding, see *The Method Of The Ruchira Avatar—The Seventeen Companions Of The True Dawn Horse, Book Five: The Divine Way Of Adidam Is An ego-Transcending Relationship, Not An ego-Centric Technique*, Part Three.

12. In this verse, Avatar Adi Da Proclaims His Identity as the Divine Person, the "Param-" ("Supreme", or "First") Avatar, the Avataric Incarnation (the original, or first, complete Descent of the Divine Person), and as the "Santosha Avatar".

"Santosha" is Sanskrit for "satisfaction" or "contentment", qualities associated with a sense of completion. These qualities are characteristics of "no-seeking", the fundamental Principle of Avatar Adi Da's Wisdom-Teaching and of His entire Revelation of Truth. Because of its uniquely appropriate meanings, "Santosha" is one of Avatar Adi Da's Names. As the Santosha Avatar, Avatar Adi Da is the Very Incarnation of Perfect Divine Contentedness, or Perfect Searchlessness.

13. In Sanskrit, "Ruchira" means "bright, radiant, effulgent". Thus, the Reference "Ruchira Avatar" indicates that Avatar Adi Da Samraj is the "Bright" (or Radiant) Descent of the Divine Reality Itself (or the Divine Truth Itself, Which Is the Only Real God) into the conditional worlds, Appearing here in bodily (human) Form.

14. Avatar Adi Da Samraj is the Divine World-Teacher because His Wisdom-Teaching is the uniquely Perfect Instruction to <u>every</u> being—in this (and every) world—in the total process of Divine Enlightenment. Furthermore, Avatar Adi Da Samraj constantly Extends His Regard to the entire world (and the entire Cosmic domain)—not on the political or social level, but as a Spiritual matter, constantly Working to Bless and Purify all beings everywhere.

15. "The 'late-time', or 'dark' epoch" is a phrase that Avatar Adi Da uses to Describe the present era, in which doubt of God (and of anything at all beyond mortal existence) is more and more pervading the entire world, and in which the separate and separative ego-"I", which is the root of all suffering and conflict, is regarded to be the ultimate principle of life.

16. Just as the traditional term "Avatar", when rightly understood, is an appropriate Reference to Avatar Adi Da Samraj, so is the traditional term "Buddha". This verse is Avatar Adi Da's Revelation that He is the Divine Buddha, the One Who Is Most Perfectly Self-Enlightened and Eternally Awake.

The Buddha-Avatar: The Divine Person, having "Crossed Down", and Appearing as the Supremely Enlightened One. This Title indicates Avatar Adi Da's Encompassing and Surpassing of the traditions of Buddhism (as a whole) and Hinduism (in particular, the school of Advaita Vedanta)—the two traditions within the collective Great Tradition of mankind that He has acknowledged as representing the highest degree of Realization known previous to His Appearance and His Revelation of the Way of Adidam. (For Avatar Adi Da's Discussion of the unique position of Buddhism and Advaita Vedanta within the Great Tradition, see *The Seven Stages Of Life*, "'God'-Talk, Real-God-Realization, and Most Perfect Divine Awakening".)

The Ruchira Buddha: The Enlightened One Who Shines with the Divine "Brightness".

The Adi-Buddha: The First (or Original) Enlightened One.

The Ati-Buddha: The Ultimate (or Highest, or Unsurpassed) Enlightened One.

The Parama-Buddha: The Supreme Buddha.

The Purushottama Buddha: "Purushottama" is a Hindu name for the Divine Person. "Uttama" means "Supreme", and "Purusha" is "Person". Therefore, the Purushottama Buddha is the Enlightened One Who Is the Supreme Divine Person. Like "Buddha-Avatar", "Purushottama Buddha" conveys Avatar Adi Da's Encompassing and Surpassing of the traditions of Buddhism and Hinduism (and, thus, the entire collective Great Tradition of mankind).

The Paramadvaita Buddha: "Advaita" means "Non-Dual". Therefore, the Paramadvaita Buddha is the One of Supreme Non-Dual Enlightenment.

The Advaitayana Buddha: "Advaitayana" means "the Vehicle of the Non-Dual Truth". The Advaitayana Buddha is the Enlightened One Who has Revealed and Given the Vehicle of Non-Dual Truth. "Advaitayana Buddhism" is another name for the Way of Adidam. (For Avatar Adi Da's discussion of "Advaitayana Buddhism", see *The Only Complete Way To Realize The Unbroken Light Of Real God—The Seventeen Companions Of The True Dawn Horse, Book Three: An Introductory Overview Of The "Radical" Divine Way Of The True World-Religion Real God Of Adidam*, Part Two, section I.)

The Ashvamedha Buddha: "Ashvamedha" means "Horse-Sacrifice", and is the name of the most revered and most mysterious of the ancient Vedic rituals. Avatar Adi Da has Revealed that the ultimate significance of this ritual is as a prayer-prophecy invoking the Avataric Descent of the Divine Person into the world, because it was intuitively understood that only the Divine Person is able to Liberate beings. Thus, the Ashvamedha Buddha is the Enlightened One Who has Submitted to be the humanly Incarnate Means for the Divine Liberation of all beings. (Avatar Adi Da's Essay on the Ashvamedha as a description and prophecy of His own Life and Work is "The True Dawn Horse Is the Only Way to Me", which appears in three Books: as the Epilogue of *The All-Completing and Final Divine Revelation To Mankind—The Seventeen Companions Of The True Dawn Horse, Book Eleven: A Summary Description Of The Supreme Yoga Of The Seventh Stage Of Life In The Divine Way Of Adidam*, as Part One of *The Heart Of The Dawn Horse Testament Of The Ruchira Avatar—The Seventeen Companions Of The True Dawn Horse, Book Twelve: The Epitome Of The "Testament Of Secrets" Of The Divine World-Teacher, Ruchira*

Avatar Adi Da Samraj, and as Part One of *The Dawn Horse Testament Of The Ruchira Avatar*.

17. This verse is Avatar Adi Da's Revelation of Himself as the Supreme Guru, or the Divine Heart-Master. Esoterically, the word "guru" is understood to be a composite of two words, "destroyer (ru) of darkness (gu)".

The Guru-Avatar: The Divine Person, having "Crossed Down" and Appearing as the Supreme Guru.

The Ruchira-Guru: The "Bright" Guru.

The Adi-Guru: The First (or Original, or Primordial) Guru.

The Ati-Guru: The Ultimate (or Highest, or Unsurpassed) Guru.

The Divine Parama-Guru: The Supreme Divine Guru.

The Purushottama-Guru: The Supreme Divine Person as Guru.

The Paramadvaita-Guru: The Supreme Non-Dual Guru.

The Advaitayana-Guru: The Guru Who has Revealed and Given the Non-Dual Vehicle.

The Ashvamedha-Guru: The Guru Who is the Divine Sacrifice and (therefore) the Means for the Divine Liberation of all beings.

18. The Sanskrit word "Siddha" means "a completed, fulfilled, or perfected one", or "one of perfect accomplishment, or power". The "Maha-Siddha" is the greatest Siddha.

The Adepts of what Avatar Adi Da calls "the 'Crazy Wisdom' tradition" (of which He is the supreme, seventh stage exemplar) are Realizers of the fourth, fifth, or sixth stages of life in any culture or time who, through spontaneous Free action, blunt Wisdom, and liberating laughter, shock or humor people into self-critical awareness of their egoity, which is a prerequisite for receiving the Realizer's Spiritual Transmission. Typically, such Realizers manifest "Crazy" activity only occasionally or temporarily, and never for its own sake but only as "skillful means".

Avatar Adi Da Himself has always addressed the ego in a unique "Crazy-Wise" manner, theatrically dramatizing, and poking fun at, the self-contracted habits, predilections, and destinies of His devotees. His "Crazy-Wise" Manner is a Divine Siddhi, an inherent aspect of His Avataric Incarnation. Through His "Crazy-Wise" Speech and Action, Avatar Adi Da Penetrates the being and loosens the patterns of ego-bondage (individually and collectively) in His devotees. The "Shock" of Truth Delivered via His "Crazy Wisdom" humbles and opens the heart, making way for the deeper reception of His Spiritual Blessing.

19. Avatar Adi Da uses the phrase "Most Perfect(ly)" in the sense of "Absolutely Perfect(ly)". Similarly, the phrase "Most Ultimate(ly)" is equivalent to "Absolutely Ultimate(ly)". "Most Perfect(ly)" and "Most Ultimate(ly)" are always references to the seventh (or Divinely Enlightened) stage of life. (See note 22.)

20. "Hridaya-Samartha Sat-Guru" is a compound of traditional San-skrit terms that has been newly created to express the uniqueness of Avatar Adi Da's Guru-Function. "Sat" means "Truth", "Being", "Exis-tence". Thus, "Sat-Guru" literally means "True Guru", or a Guru who can lead living beings from darkness (or non-Truth) into Light (or the Living Truth).

"Samartha" means "fit", "qualified", "able". Thus, "Samartha-Sat-Guru" means "a True Guru who is fully capable" of Awakening living beings to Real-God-Realization.

The word "Hridaya", meaning "heart", refers to the Very Heart, or the Transcendental (and Inherently Spiritual) Divine Reality.

Thus, altogether, the reference "Hridaya-Samartha Sat-Guru" means "the Divine Heart-Master Who Liberates His devotees from the darkness of egoity by Means of the Power of the 'Bright' Divine Heart Itself". Avatar Adi Da has said that this full Designation "properly summarizes all the aspects of My unique Guru-Function".

21. On January 11, 1986, Avatar Adi Da passed through a profound Yogic Swoon, which He later Described as the initial Event of His Divine "Emergence". Avatar Adi Da's Divine "Emergence" is an ongo-ing Process in which His bodily (human) Form has been (and is ever more profoundly and potently being) conformed to Himself, the Very Divine Person, such that His bodily (human) Form is now (and for-ever hereafter) an utterly Unobstructed Sign and Agent of His own Divine Being.

For Avatar Adi Da's Revelation of the significance of His Divine "Emergence", see section III of "The True Dawn Horse Is The Only Way To Me" (which Essay appears as the Epilogue of *The All-Com-pleting and Final Divine Revelation To Mankind*, as Part One of *The Heart Of The Dawn Horse Testament Of The Ruchira Avatar*, and as Part One of *The Dawn Horse Testament Of The Ruchira Avatar*).

22. Avatar Adi Da has Revealed the underlying structure of human growth in seven stages.

The first three stages of life develop, respectively, the physical, emotional, and mental/volitional functions of the body-mind. The first stage begins at birth and continues for approximately five to seven years; the second stage follows, continuing until approximately the age of twelve to fourteen; and the third stage is optimally complete by the early twenties. In the case of virtually all individuals, however, failed adaptation in the earlier stages of life means that maturity in the third stage of life takes much longer to attain, and it is usually never fulfilled, with the result that the ensuing stages of Spiritual development do not even begin.

In the Way of Adidam, however, growth in the first three stages of life unfolds in the Spiritual Company of Avatar Adi Da and is based in the practice of feeling-Contemplation of His bodily (human) Form and in devotion, service, and self-discipline in relation to His bodily (human) Form. By the Grace of this relationship to Avatar Adi Da, the first three (or foundation) stages of life are lived and fulfilled in a self-transcending devotional disposition, or (as He Describes it) "in the 'original' or beginner's devotional context of the fourth stage of life".

The fourth stage of life is the transitional stage between the gross, bodily-based point of view of the first three stages of life and the subtle, psychic point of view of the fifth stage of life. The fourth stage of life is the stage of Spiritual devotion, or surrender of separate self, in which the gross functions of the being are submitted to the higher psychic, or subtle, functions of the being, and, through these psychic functions, to the Divine. In the fourth stage of life, the gross, or bodily-based, personality of the first three stages of life is purified through reception of the Spiritual Force ("Holy Spirit", or "Shakti") of the Divine Reality, Which prepares the being to out-grow the bodily-based point of view.

In the Way of Adidam, as the orientation of the fourth stage of life matures, heart-felt surrender to the bodily (human) Form of Avatar Adi Da deepens by His Grace, drawing His devotee into Love-Communion with His All-Pervading Spiritual Presence. Growth in the "basic" context of the fourth stage of life in the Way of the Heart is also characterized by a Baptizing Current of Spirit-Energy that is at first felt to flow down the front of the body from above the head to the bodily base.

The Descent of Avatar Adi Da's Spirit-Baptism releases obstructions predominantly in the waking, or frontal, personality. This frontal Yoga purifies His devotee and infuses him or her with His Spirit-Power. Avatar Adi Da's devotee is awakened to profound love of and devotional intimacy with Him.

If the transition to the sixth stage of life is not otherwise made at maturity in the "basic" context of the fourth stage of life, the Spirit-Current is felt to turn about at the bodily base and ascend to the brain core, and the fourth stage of life matures to its "advanced" context, which involves the ascent of Avatar Adi Da's Spiritual Blessing and purifies the spinal line of the body-mind.

In the fifth stage of life, attention is concentrated in the subtle, or psychic, levels of awareness in ascent. The Spirit-Current is felt to penetrate the brain core and rise toward the Matrix of Light and Love-Bliss infinitely above the crown of the head, possibly culminating in the temporary experience of fifth stage conditional Nirvikalpa Samadhi, or "formless ecstasy". In the Way of the Heart, most practitioners will not need to practice in the context of the fifth stage of life, but will rather be Awakened, by Adi Da's Grace, from maturity in the fourth stage of life to the Witness-Position of Consciousness (in the context of the sixth stage of life).

In the traditional development of the sixth stage of life, attention is inverted upon the essential self and the Perfectly Subjective Position of Consciousness, to the exclusion of conditional phenomena. In the Way of the Heart, however, the deliberate intention to invert attention for the sake of Realizing Transcendental Consciousness does not characterize the sixth stage of life, which instead begins when the Witness-Position of Consciousness spontaneously Awakens and becomes stable.

In the course of the sixth stage of life, the mechanism of attention, which is the root-action of egoity (felt as separation, self-contraction, or the feeling of relatedness), gradually subsides. In the fullest context of the sixth stage of life, the knot of attention dissolves and all sense of relatedness yields to the Blissful and undifferentiated Feeling of Being. The characteristic Samadhi of the sixth stage of life is Jnana Samadhi, the temporary and exclusive Realization of the Transcendental Self, or Consciousness Itself.

The transition from the sixth stage of life to the seventh stage Realization of Absolute Non-Separateness is the unique Revelation of Avatar Adi Da. Various traditions and individuals previous to Adi Da's Revelation have had sixth stage intuitions or premonitions of the Most Perfect seventh stage Realization, but no one previous to Avatar Adi Da has Realized the seventh stage of life.

The seventh stage Realization is the Gift of Avatar Adi Da to His devotees, Awakened only in the context of the Way of Adidam that He has Revealed and Given. The seventh stage of life begins when His devotee Awakens, by His Grace, from the exclusive Realization of Consciousness to Most Perfect and permanent Identification with Consciousness Itself, Avatar Adi Da's Very (and Inherently Perfect) State. This is Divine Self-Realization, or Divine Enlightenment, the perpetual Samadhi of "Open Eyes" (seventh stage Sahaj Samadhi), in which all "things" are Divinely Recognized without "difference" as merely apparent modifications of the One Self-Existing and Self-Radiant Divine Consciousness. In the course of the seventh stage of life, there may be spontaneous incidents in which psycho-physical states and phenomena do not appear to the notice, being Outshined by the "Bright" Radiance of Consciousness Itself. This Samadhi, which is the ultimate Realization of Divine Existence, culminates in Divine Translation, or the permanent Outshining of all apparent conditions in the Inherently Perfect Radiance and Love-Bliss of the Divine Self-Condition.

In the context of practice of the Way of Adidam, the seven stages of life as Revealed by Avatar Adi Da are not a version of the traditional "ladder" of Spiritual attainment. These stages and their characteristic signs arise naturally in the course of practice for a fully practicing devotee in the Way of Adidam, but the practice itself is oriented to the transcendence of the first six stages of life, in the seventh stage Disposition of Inherently Liberated Happiness, Granted by Avatar Adi Da's Grace in His Love-Blissful Spiritual Company.

For Avatar Adi Da's extended Instruction relative to the seven stages of life, see *The Seven Stages Of Life—The Seventeen Companions Of The True Dawn Horse, Book Ten: Transcending The Six Stages Of egoic Life and Realizing The ego-Transcending Seventh Stage Of Life In The Divine Way Of Adidam.*

23. This verse is Avatar Adi Da's Self-Revelation as the Supreme Avatar.

The Ruchira Buddha-Avatar: The "Bright" Enlightened One Who is the Incarnation of the Divine Person.

The Tathagata Avatar: "Tathagata" means "One who has thus gone". It is a title traditionally given to Gautama Shakyamuni and other Buddhas. Like "Buddha-Avatar" and "Purushottama Buddha", "Tathagata Avatar" conveys Avatar Adi Da's Encompassing and Surpassing of the traditions of Buddhism and Hinduism (and, thus, the entire collective Great Tradition of mankind).

The Hridaya Avatar: "Hridaya" is Sanskrit for "the heart". It refers not only to the physical organ but also to the True Heart, the Transcendental (and Inherently Spiritual) Divine Reality. "Hridaya" in combination with "Avatar" signifies that Avatar Adi Da is the Very Incarnation of the Divine Heart Itself, the Divine Incarnation Who Stands in, at, and As the True Heart of every being.

The Love-Ananda Avatar: The Name "Love-Ananda" combines both English ("Love") and Sanskrit ("Ananda", meaning "Bliss"), thus bridging the West and the East, and communicating Avatar Adi Da's Function as the Divine World-Teacher. The combination of "Love" and "Ananda" means "the Divine Love-Bliss". The Name "Love-Ananda" was given to Avatar Adi Da by His principal human Spiritual Master, Swami Muktananda, who spontaneously conferred it upon Avatar Adi

Da in 1969. However, Avatar Adi Da did not use the Name "Love-Ananda" until April 1986, after the Great Event that Initiated His Divine "Emergence". As the Love-Ananda Avatar, Avatar Adi Da is the Very Incarnation of the Divine Love-Bliss.

The Avabhasa Avatar: The Sanskrit word "Avabhasa" has a rich range of associations. It means "brightness", "appearance", "manifestation", "splendor", "lustre", "light", "knowledge". Its verb root may be interpreted as "shining toward", "shining down", "showing oneself". It is thus synonymous with the English term "the 'Bright'", which Avatar Adi Da has used since His childhood to Describe the Blissfully Self-Luminous Divine Being That He knew even then as the All-Pervading, Transcendental, Inherently Spiritual, and Divine Reality of His own body-mind and of all beings, things, and worlds. As the Avabhasa Avatar, Avatar Adi Da is the Very Incarnation of the Divine Self-"Brightness".

24. Avatar Adi Da Samraj Speaks of the Way of Adidam as a "Pleasure Dome", recalling the poem "Kubla Khan", by Samuel Taylor Coleridge ("In Xanadu did Kubla Khan/A stately pleasure-dome decree . . ."). Adi Da Samraj points out that in many religious traditions it is presumed that one must embrace suffering in order to earn future happiness and pleasure. However, by Calling His devotees to live the Way of Adidam as a Pleasure Dome, Avatar Adi Da Samraj Communicates His Teaching that the Way of heart-Communion with Him is always about present-time Happiness, not about any kind of search to attain Happiness in the future. Thus, in the Way of Adidam, there is no idealization of suffering and pain as presumed means to attain future happiness. Therefore, in the Way of Adidam, there is no denial of the appropriate enjoyment of even the ordinary pleasures of human life.

In this passage, Avatar Adi Da uses "Pleasure Dome" as a reference to the Ultimate and Divine Love-Bliss-Happiness That is His own Self-Nature and His Gift to all who respond to Him.

25. When Consciousness is free of identification with the body-mind, it takes up its natural "position" as the Conscious Witness of all that arises to and in and as the body-mind.

In the Way of Adidam, the stable Realization of the Witness-Position is associated with, or demonstrated via, the effortless surrender (or relaxation) of all the forms of seeking and all the motives of attention that characterize the first five stages of life. However, identification with the Witness-Position is not final (or Most Perfect) Realization of the Divine Self. Rather, it is the first of the three stages of the "Perfect Practice" in the Way of Adidam, which Practice, in due course, Realizes, by Avatar Adi Da's Liberating Grace, complete and irreversible and utterly Love-Blissful Identification with Consciousness Itself.

26. "Listening" is Avatar Adi Da's technical term for the orientation, disposition, and beginning practice of the Way of Adidam. A listening devotee "listens" to Avatar Adi Da Samraj by "considering" His Teaching Argument and His Leelas, and by practicing feeling-Contemplation of Him (primarily of His bodily human Form). In the total (or full and complete) practice of the Way of Adidam, effective listening is the necessary prerequisite for true hearing and true seeing (see note 27).

"Hearing" is a technical term used by Avatar Adi Da to Describe most fundamental understanding of the act of egoity (or self-contraction). Hearing is the unique capability to directly transcend the self-contraction, such that, simultaneous with that transcendence, there is the intuitive awakening to the Revelation of the Divine Person and Self-Condition. The capability of true hearing can only be Granted by Avatar Adi Da's Grace, to His fully practicing devotee who has effectively completed the process of listening. Only on the basis of such hearing can Spiritually Awakened practice of the Way of Adidam truly (or with full responsibility) begin.

I Am Heard When My Listening Devotee Has Truly (and Thoroughly) Observed the ego-"I" and Understood it (Directly, In the moments Of self-Observation, and Most Fundamentally, or In its Totality).

I Am Heard When the ego-"I" Is Altogether (and Thoroughly) Observed and (Most Fundamentally) Understood, Both In The Tendency To Dissociate and In The Tendency To Become Attached (or To Cling By Wanting Need, or To Identify With others, and things, and circumstances egoically, and Thus To Dramatize The Seeker, Bereft Of Basic Equanimity, Wholeness, and The Free Capability For Simple Relatedness).

I Am Heard When the ego-"I" Is Thoroughly (and Most Fundamentally) Understood To Be Contraction-Only, An Un-Necessary and Destructive Motive and Design, Un-Naturally and Chronically Added To Cosmic Nature and To all relations, and An Imaginary Heart-Disease (Made To Seem Real, By Heart-Reaction).

I Am Heard When This Most Fundamental Understanding Of The Habit Of "Narcissus" Becomes The Directly Obvious Realization Of The Heart, Radiating Beyond Its Own (Apparent) Contraction.

I Am Heard When The Beginning Is Full, and The Beginning Is Full (and Ended) When Every Gesture Of self-Contraction (In The Context Of The First Three Stages Of Life, and Relative To Each and

All Of The Principal Faculties, Of body, emotion, mind, and breath) Is (As A Rather Consistently Applied and humanly Effective Discipline) Observed (By Natural feeling-perception), Tacitly (and Most Fundamentally) Understood, and Really (Directly and Effectively) Felt Beyond (In The Prior Feeling Of Unqualified Relatedness). (The Dawn Horse Testament Of The Ruchira Avatar, chapter nineteen)

For Avatar Adi Da's fundamental Instruction relative to the listening-hearing process, see chapter nineteen of *The Dawn Horse Testament Of The Ruchira Avatar*, or chapters twenty-one through twenty-three of *The Heart Of The Dawn Horse Testament Of The Ruchira Avatar*.

27. When, in the practice of the Way of Adidam, hearing (or most fundamental self-understanding) is steadily exercised in meditation and in life, the native feeling of the heart ceases to be chronically constricted by self-contraction. The heart then begins to Radiate as love in response to the Spiritual (and Always Blessing) Presence of Avatar Adi Da.

This emotional and Spiritual response of the whole being is what Avatar Da calls "seeing". Seeing is emotional conversion from the reactive emotions that characterize egoic self-obsession, to the open-hearted, Radiant Happiness that characterizes God-Love and Spiritual devotion to Avatar Adi Da. This true and stable emotional conversion coincides with true and stable receptivity to Avatar Adi Da's Spiritual Transmission, and both of these are prerequisites to further Spiritual advancement in the Way of Adidam.

Seeing Is self-Transcending Participation In <u>What</u> (and <u>Who</u>) Is. Seeing Is Love. Seeing, or Love, Is Able (By My Grace) To "Locate", Recognize, and Feel My All-Pervading Spiritual Radiance (and My Spirit-Identity, <u>As</u> The Divine Person, or The "Bright" and Only One <u>Who</u> Is). Therefore, Seeing Is Heart-Felt and Whole bodily Identification Of The Love-Bliss-Presence and Person (or Mere Being) Of The Divine. Seeing Is Spiritually Activated Conversion Of attention, emotion, and the Total psycho-physical personality From self-Contraction To The Spiritual Form (or Tangible Spiritual Presence) Of Real God (or The Necessarily Divine Reality and Truth, Itself), and This Via My Spirit-Baptism (or Divine and Inherently Perfect Hridaya-Shaktipat, or Divine and Inherently Perfect Heart-Awakening, and The Subsequent Apparent Descent and Circulation Of The Divine Spirit-Force Into and Through and, Ultimately, Beyond the body-mind Of My Progressively Awakening Devotee). Seeing Is Spontaneous (or Heart-Moved) Devotional Sacrifice Of the self-Contraction. Seeing Is The "Radical" (or Directly self-Transcending) Reorientation Of conditional Existence To The Transcendental, Inherently Spiritual, and Inherently Perfect Divine Self-Condi-

tion (and Source-Condition) In Whom (or In Which) conditional self and conditional worlds Apparently arise and Always Already Inhere.

Seeing, Like Hearing, Is A "Radical" (or "Gone To The Root, Core, Source, or Origin") Capability That Can and Should Be Exercised moment to moment. When There Is (In any moment) Real Seeing Of Me, There Is The Capability To Contact Me Spiritually and Enter Into Communion With Me Spiritually. When You Have Awakened (By My Grace) To See Me Truly, Then The Act (and Sadhana) Of Contacting Me Spiritually Does Not, In *every* moment Of Its Exercise, Require That You Come Into The Physical Sphere Of My Bodily (Human) Form (or, After The Physical Lifetime Of My Bodily Human Form, Into The physical Sphere Of My "Living Murti") or That You Enter Into a place Spiritually Empowered By Me. My Devotee Who Sees Me Is (In The General Course Of moment to moment Practice Of Devotion To Me) Capable Of Contacting Me Spiritually In any circumstance, By Using The "Radical" Virtue Of Hearing and Seeing To Go Beyond The self-Contracting Tendency.

Seeing Is Simply Attraction To Me, and Feeling Me, As My Spiritual (and Always Blessing) Presence, and This Most Fundamentally, At The Root, Core, Source, or Origin Of The Emergence Of My Presence "here" (At and In Front Of The Heart, or At and In The Root-Context Of the body-mind, or At and In The Source-Position, and, Ultimately, As The Source-Condition, Of conditional, or psycho-physical, Existence Itself).

Seeing Is Knowing Me As My Spiritual (and Always Blessing) Presence, Just As Tangibly, and With The Same Degree Of Clarity, As You Would Differentiate The Physical Appearance Of My Bodily (Human) Form From the physical appearance of the bodily (human) form of any other.

To See Me Is A Clear and "Radical" Knowledge Of Me, About Which There Is No Doubt. To See Me Is A Sudden, Tacit Awareness, Like Walking Into a "thicker" air or atmosphere, or Suddenly Feeling a breeze, or Jumping Into water and Noticing The Difference In Density Between the air and the water. This Tangible Feeling Of Me Is (In any particular moment) Not Necessarily (Otherwise) Associated With effects in the body-mind . . . , but It Is, Nevertheless, Felt At The Heart and Even All Over the body.

Seeing Me Is One-Pointedness In The "Radical" Conscious Process Of Heart-Devotion To Me. (The Dawn Horse Testament Of The Ruchira Avatar, chapter twenty)

For Avatar Adi Da's fundamental Instruction relative to seeing, see chapter twenty of *The Dawn Horse Testament Of The Ruchira Avatar*, or chapters twenty-four through twenty-eight of *The Heart Of The Dawn Horse Testament Of The Ruchira Avatar*.

28. Avatar Adi Da Samraj spontaneously Gave the Name "Adidam" in January 1996. This primary Name for the Way He has Revealed and Given is simply His own Principal Name ("Adi Da") with the addition of "m" at the end. When He first Gave this Name, Adi Da Samraj pointed out that the final "m" adds a mantric force, evoking the effect of the primal Sanskrit syllable "Om". (For Avatar Adi Da's Revelation of the most profound esoteric significance of "Om" as the Divine Sound of His own Very Being, see *He-and-She Is Me—The Seventeen Companions Of The True Dawn Horse, Book Seven: The Indivisibility Of Consciousness and Light In The Divine Body Of The Ruchira Avatar.*) Simultaneously, the final "m" suggests the English word "Am" (expressing "I Am"), such that the Name "Adidam" also evokes Avatar Adi Da's Primal Self-Confession, "I Am Adi Da", or, more simply, "I Am Da" (or "Aham Da Asmi").

29. Avatar Adi Da has indicated that all practitioners of the Way of Adidam, whatever their form or developmental stage of practice, may, at any time, Remember and Invoke Him (or feel, and thereby Contemplate, His bodily human Form, His Spiritual, and Always Blessing, Presence, and His Very, and Inherently Perfect, State) via simple heart-feeling and by randomly, in daily life and meditation, reciting His Principal Name, "Da", or any other of His Names which He has Given for the practice of simple Name-Invocation of Him. (The forms of simple Name-Invocation are Given in chapter three of *The Dawn Horse Testament Of The Ruchira Avatar.*)

30. A "mudra" is a gesture of the hands, face, or body that outwardly expresses a state of ecstasy. Even in His Divine State of Being Itself, Avatar Adi Da may spontaneously exhibit Mudras as Signs of His Blessing and Purifying Work with His devotees. Here He is speaking of the Attitude of His Blessing Work, which is His Constant (or Eternal) Giving, or Submitting, of Himself to Be the Means of Liberation for all beings.

31. The Sanskrit word "hridayam" (meaning "heart") refers not only to the physical organ but also to the True Heart, the Transcendental (and Inherently Spiritual) Divine Reality Itself. "Hridayam" is one of Avatar Adi Da's Divine Names, signifying (as explained in this passage) that He Stands In, At, and As the True Heart of every being.

32. "Dau Loloma" is Avatar Adi Da's primary Fijian Name, which literally means "the Adept (Dau) of Love (Loloma)". This Name was given to Avatar Adi Da by native Fijians soon after He first arrived in Fiji in 1983.

33. "Vunirarama", Fijian for "the Source of 'Brightness'" ("Vu" means "source" or "origin", "ni" means "of", and "rarama" means "bright-

ness") can be used as an extension of Avatar Adi Da's Fijian Name, "Dau Loloma". This Name was given to Avatar Adi Da Samraj in 1991 by Fijians who live and serve at His Island-Hermitage, Adidam Samrajashram (the Fijian Island of Naitauba).

34. "Turaga" is Fijian for "Lord". This Title was offered to Avatar Adi Da by a native Fijian in 1993.

35. "Tui" is Fijian for "Great Chief". This Title was offered to Avatar Adi Da by the native Fijians immediately upon His arrival at Naitauba in 1983.

36. "Samraj" is a traditional term used to refer to great kings, but also to refer to the Hindu gods. In Sanskrit, "Samraja" is defined as "universal or supreme ruler", "paramount Lord", or "paramount sovereign".

   The Sanskrit word "raja" (the basic root of "Samraj") means "king". It comes from the verbal root "raj", meaning "to reign, to rule, to illuminate". The prefix "sam-" expresses "union" or "completeness". "Samraj" is thus literally the complete ruler, the ruler of everything altogether. "Samraj" was traditionally given as a title to a king who was considered to be a "universal monarch".

   Avatar Adi Da's Name "Adi Da Samraj" expresses that He is the Primordial (or Original) Giver, Who Blesses all as the Universal Ruler of every thing, every where, for all time. The Sovereignty of His Kingdom has nothing to do with the world of human politics. Rather, it is entirely a matter of His Spiritual Dominion over all and All, His Kingship in the hearts of His devotees.

37. The Feeling of Being is the uncaused (or Self-Existing), Self-Radiant, and unqualified feeling-intuition of the Transcendental, Inherently Spiritual, and Divine Self. This absolute Feeling does not merely accompany or express the Realization of the Heart Itself, but It is Identical to that Realization. To feel—or, really, to Be—the Feeling of Being is to enjoy the Love-Bliss of Absolute Consciousness, Which, when Most Perfectly Realized, cannot be prevented or even diminished either by the events of life or by death.

38. For devotees of Avatar Adi Da Samraj, His Names are the Names of the Very Divine Being. As such, these Names, as Avatar Adi Da Himself has Described, "do not simply mean Real God, or the Blessing of Real God. They are the verbal or audible Form of the Divine." Therefore, Invoking Avatar Adi Da Samraj by Name is a potent and Divinely Empowered form of feeling-Contemplation of Him.

Part Two

39. Avatar Adi Da uses the terms "Spiritual", "Transcendental", and "Divine" in reference to different dimensions of Reality that are Realized progressively in the Way of Adidam. "Spiritual" refers to the reception of the Spirit-Force (in the "basic" and "advanced" contexts of the fourth stage of life and in the context of the fifth stage of life); "Transcendental" refers to the Realization of Consciousness Itself as separate from the world (in the context of the sixth stage of life); and "Divine" refers to the Most Perfect Realization of Consciousness Itself as utterly Non-separate from the world (in the context of the seventh stage of life). (For Avatar Adi Da's fully extended discussion of the stages of life, see *The Seven Stages Of Life*.)

40. See note 22.

41. The Sanskrit word "Samadhi" traditionally denotes various exalted states that appear in the context of esoteric meditation and Realization. Avatar Adi Da Teaches that, in the Way of Adidam, Samadhi is, even more simply and fundamentally, a state of ego-transcendence in heart-Communion with Him, and that "the cultivation of Samadhi" is another way to describe the practice of Ruchira Avatara Bhakti Yoga that is the fundamental basis of the Way of Adidam. Avatar Adi Da's devotee is in Samadhi in any moment of standing beyond the separate self in true devotional heart-Communion with Him. (See "The Cultivation of My Divine Samadhi", in *The Seven Stages Of Life*.)

   The developmental process leading to Divine Enlightenment in the Way of Adidam may be marked by many signs, principal among which are the Samadhis of the advanced and the ultimate stages of life and practice. Although some of the "Great Samadhis" of the fourth, the fifth, and the sixth stages of life may appear in the course of an individual's practice of the Way of Adidam, the appearance of all of them is by no means necessary, or even probable, as Avatar Adi Da indicates in His Wisdom-Teaching. All the possible forms of Samadhi in the Way of Adidam are described in full detail in *The Dawn Horse Testament Of The Ruchira Avatar*.

42. Avatar Adi Da uses the term "bond", when lower-cased, to refer to the process by which the egoic individual (already presuming separateness and, therefore, bondage to the separate self) attaches itself karmically to the world of others and things through the constant search for self-fulfillment. In contrast, when He capitalizes the term "Bond", Avatar Adi Da is making reference to the process of His devotee's devotional "Bonding" to Him, which process is the Great Means for transcending all forms of limited, or karmic, "bonding".

43. "Leela" is Sanskrit for "play", or "sport". In many religious and Spiritual traditions, all of conditionally manifested existence is regarded to be the Leela (or the Divine Play, Sport, or Free Activity) of the Divine Person. "Leela" also means the Awakened Play of a Realized Adept of any degree, through which he or she mysteriously Instructs and Liberates others and Blesses the world itself. By extension, a Leela is an instructive and inspiring story of such an Adept's Teaching and Blessing Play.

44. "Murti" is Sanskrit for "form", and, by extension, a "representational image" of the Divine or of a Guru. In the Way of Adidam, Murtis of Avatar Adi Da are most commonly photographs of Avatar Adi Da's bodily (human) Form.

45. Avatar Adi Da has said that, after His physical (human) Lifetime, there should always be one (and only one) "Living Murti" as a Living Link between Him and His devotees. Each successive "Living Murti" (or "Murti-Guru") is to be selected from among those members of the Ruchira Sannyasin Order (the senior renunciate order of Adidam, see pp. 175-77 for full description) who have been formally acknowledged as Divinely Enlightened devotees of Avatar Adi Da Samraj in the seventh stage of life. "Living Murtis" will not function as the independent Gurus of practitioners of the Way of Adidam. Rather, they will simply be "Representations" of Avatar Adi Da's bodily (human) Form, and a means to Commune with Him.

For a full discussion of "Living Murtis", or "Murti-Gurus", and how they are chosen, see chapter twenty of *The Dawn Horse Testament Of The Ruchira Avatar*.

46. Avatar Adi Da Affirms that there is a Divine Self-Domain that is the Perfectly Subjective Condition of the conditional worlds. It is not "elsewhere", not an objective "place" (like a subtle "heaven" or mythical "paradise"), but It is the always present, Transcendental, Inherently Spiritual, Divine Source-Condition of every conditionally manifested being and thing. Avatar Adi Da Reveals that the Divine Self-Domain is not other than the Divine Heart Itself, Who He <u>Is</u>. To Realize the seventh stage of life (by the Grace of Avatar Adi Da Samraj) is to Awaken to the Divine Self-Domain.

47. Avatar Adi Da has Revealed that there are two fundamental aspects of His Divine Blessing—His Fiery, Purifying Force, and His Gentle, Nurturing Force, both of which are manifestations of His Overwhelming Love of all beings. He has indicated that these aspects

of His Blessing are associated with the two sides of His physical Body, and particularly with His Feet. Thus, His right Foot (on the "yang" side of the body) is His "Power Foot", associated with His Force of Expectation and Demand, and His left Foot (on the "yin" side of the body) is His "Beauty Foot", associated with the Sweetness of His Love and Blessing.

What You Can Do Next

Contact one of our centers.

■ Sign up for our preliminary course, "The <u>Only</u> Truth That Sets The Heart Free". This course will prepare you to become a fully practicing devotee of Avatar Adi Da Samraj.

■ Or sign up for any of our other classes, seminars, events, or retreats, or for a study course available by correspondence:

AMERICAS
12040 North Seigler Road
Middletown, CA 95461
(800) 524-4941
(707) 928-4936

PACIFIC-ASIA
12 Seibel Road
Henderson
Auckland 1008
New Zealand
64-9-838-9114

AUSTRALIA
P.O. Box 460
Roseville, NSW 2069
Australia
61-2-9416-7951

EUROPE-AFRICA
Annendaalderweg 10
6105 AT Maria Hoop
The Netherlands
31 (0)20 468 1442

THE UNITED KINGDOM
London, England
0181-7317550

E-MAIL: correspondence@adidam.org

Read these books by and about the Divine World-Teacher, Ruchira Avatar Adi Da Samraj:

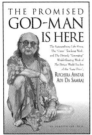

■ ***The Promised God-Man Is Here***
The Extraordinary Life-Story, The "Crazy" Teaching-Work, and The Divinely "Emerging" World-Blessing Work Of The Divine World-Teacher Of The "Late-Time", Ruchira Avatar Adi Da Samraj, by Carolyn Lee, Ph.D.—the profound, heart-rending, humorous, miraculous, wild—and true—story of the Divine Person Alive in human Form. Essential reading as background for the study of Avatar Adi Da's books.

■ ***See My Brightness Face to Face***
A Celebration of the Ruchira Avatar, Adi Da Samraj, and the First Twenty-Five Years of His Divine Revelation Work—a magnificent year-by-year pictorial celebration of Ruchira Avatar Adi Da's Divine Work with His devotees, from 1972-1997. Includes a wealth of selections from His Talks and Writings, numerous Stories of His Divine Work told by His devotees, and over 100 color photographs.

■ ***Ruchira Avatara Gita***
(The Way Of The Divine Heart-Master)
The Five Books Of The Heart Of The Adidam Revelation, Book Two: The "Late-Time" Avataric Revelation Of The Great Secret Of The Divinely Self-Revealed Way That Most Perfectly Realizes The True and Spiritual Divine Person (The egoless Personal Presence Of Reality and Truth, Which <u>Is</u> The Only <u>Real</u> God)
In this book, the second of His twenty-three "Source-Texts", Avatar Adi Da Describes, in beautifully poetic terms, the key to Liberation—the devotional relationship to Him, lived in every aspect of life.

After reading *Ruchira Avatara Gita*, continue your reading with the remaining books of *The Five Books Of The Heart Of The Adidam Revelation* (the *Da Love-Ananda Gita*, *Hridaya Rosary*, and *Eleutherios*). Then you will be ready to go on to *The Seventeen Companions Of The True Dawn Horse* (see pp. 195-99). These and other books by and about Ruchira Avatar Adi Da Samraj can be ordered directly from the Dawn Horse Press by calling:

(800) 524-4941 (from within North America)
(707) 928-4936 (from outside North America)

or by writing to:

The Dawn Horse Press
12040 North Seigler Road
Middletown, CA 95461

Or you can order these, or any of the other products distributed by the Dawn Horse Press, by visiting the Dawn Horse Press on-line at: **http://dhp.adidam.org**.

Visit our website:
http://www.adidam.org.

Our award-winning website contains a wealth of photographs of Ruchira Avatar Adi Da Samraj, audio-clips of Him Speaking, excerpts from His Writings, and recent Stories of His world-Blessing Work. The website also has a full listing of Adidam regional centers worldwide.

For a full description of all the forms of involvement in the Way of Adidam, see "Surely Come to Me" on pp. 171-91.

RUCHIRA AVATAR ADI DA SAMRAJ
Adidam Samrajashram (Naitauba), Fiji, 1997

"Surely Come to Me"

An Invitation to the Way of Adidam

*I __Am__ The Divine Heart-Master. I Take My Stand In
The Heart Of My Devotee. Have You Realized The Heart,
Who __Is__ The Mystery Of You and Me?*

How Could I Deny Heart-Vision To My Loved-One?

How Could I Delay The Course Of My Beloved?

*Like An Intimate Family Servant, I Dearly Serve My
Devotee.*

Like A Wealthy Friend, I Freely Give To My Devotee.

*Like A Mad Priest, I Even Worship My Devotee, With
Love Itself.*

*Like An Innocent Boy At First Love, I Would Awaken
My Devotee In Radiant Chambers.*

*Where The Wound Of Love Churns and Never Heals, I
Wait, Longing To Celebrate The Brilliant Sight Of My
Devotee.*

Come Slowly or Quickly, but Surely Come To Me.

*Touch My Heart, and I Will Widen You To God-
Knows-Where.*

THE DAWN HORSE TESTAMENT OF THE RUCHIRA AVATAR

You are Blessed to be alive at the time of the Greatest of Revelations—the All-Completing Revelation of Real God promised by all the religious and Spiritual traditions of mankind. The Divine World-Teacher, Ruchira Avatar Adi Da Samraj, is that All-Completing Revelation. He is the Perfect Fulfillment of that universal promise.

Ruchira Avatar Adi Da Samraj Offers you a devotional relationship which literally brings His tangible Divine Blessing into your life. For the sake of all who are moved to go beyond all the dead-ends of ordinary life and all the dead-ends of Spiritual seeking, Ruchira Avatar Adi Da

Samraj has Revealed and Given the unique Way of Adidam—the only complete Way to Realize the True and Spiritual Divine Person, Who Is Reality Itself, or Truth Itself, or Real God.

You have before you now the greatest of life-choices: How are you going to respond to the Most Perfect Revelation of Real God?

How To Respond

The Divine World-Teacher, Ruchira Avatar Adi Da Samraj, Calls you to formally become His devotee—which means to formally take up practice of the Way of Adidam, the Divinely Enlightening Way of life He has Revealed and Given for the sake of all beings.

Because those who approach Him have different heart-needs and different life-circumstances to account for, Ruchira Avatar Adi Da has created four congregations of formal approach to Him. These four congregations, together, make up the Eleutherian Pan-Communion of Adidam (or, simply, the Adidam Pan-Communion). Which of the four congregations of the Adidam Pan-Communion you should apply to for membership depends on the strength of your impulse to respond to Avatar Adi Da's Revelation and on your life-circumstance.

Take Up the Total Practice
of the Way of Adidam

(The First and Second Congregations
of the Adidam Pan-Communion)

The first and second congregations of the Adidam Pan-Communion are for practitioners of the <u>total</u> practice of the Way of Adidam (and for student-novices, who are formally approaching the total practice of the Way of Adidam). In particular, the first congregation is for those who have dedicated their lives <u>one-pointedly</u> to Realizing Real God—it is the congregation made up of the two formal renunciate orders of Adidam: the Ruchira Sannyasin Order of the Tantric Renunciates of Adidam, and the Avabhasin Lay Renunciate Order of the Tantric Renunciates of Adidam. The second congregation is made up of student-novices, student-beginners, and members of the Lay Congregationist Order of Adidam (which is the general lay practicing and serving order of Ruchira Avatar Adi Da's lay devotees who have advanced beyond the student-beginner stage).

To take up the total practice of the Way of Adidam is to take full advantage of the opportunity Offered by Ruchira Avatar Adi Da Samraj—it is to enter fully into the Process of Real-God-Realization. That Process of Real-God-Realization is a unique ordeal, which necessarily requires application to a wide range of functional, practical, relational, and cultural self-disciplines Revealed and Given by Ruchira Avatar Adi Da Samraj for the sake of that Divine Process. These disciplines allow the body-mind to be made ever more available to Ruchira Avatar Adi Da's Blessing Transmission. They range from foundation practices relative to diet, health, sexuality, and work, to the core devotional practices of meditation, sacramental worship, and study of Avatar Adi Da's Wisdom-Teaching. The Way of Adidam is not a "talking" school based on merely adhering to a certain philosophy or upholding a certain religious point of view. Rather, the Way of Adidam is a "practicing" school, in which you participate in the Process of Real-God-Realization with every aspect of your being.

If you want to enter fully into the Process of Real-God-Realization in the Company of Ruchira Avatar Adi Da Samraj, then you should apply to become a member of the second congregation of the Adidam Pan-Communion—and if you are moved to one-pointedly dedicate your life to the Process of Real-God-Realization, after a period of exemplary practice in the second congregation, you may apply to practice as a formal renunciate in the first congregation. (The life of members of the first and second congregations is described and pictured on pp. 184-88.)

When you apply for membership in the second congregation of the Adidam Pan-Communion (the first step for all who want to take up the total practice of the Way of Adidam), you will be asked to prepare yourself by taking "The Only Truth That Sets the Heart Free", a course of formal study and "consideration" (lasting four to six weeks), in which you examine the Opportunity Offered to you by Avatar Adi Da Samraj, and learn what it means to embrace the total practice of the Way of Adidam as a second-congregation devotee of Ruchira Avatar Adi Da. (To register for this preparatory course, please contact the regional or territorial center nearest to you [see p. 191], or e-mail us at: correspondence@adidam.org.) After completing this period of study, you may formally enter the second congregation by becoming a student-novice.

Entering any of the four congregations of Adidam involves taking a formal vow of devotion and service to Avatar Adi Da Samraj. This vow is a profound—and, indeed, eternal—commitment. You take this vow (for whichever congregation you are entering) when you are certain that your great and true heart-impulse is to be devoted, forever, to Avatar Adi Da Samraj as your Divine Heart-Master. If you recognize Avatar Adi Da as the Living

Divine Person—your Perfect Guide and Help and your eternal and most intimate Heart-Companion—then you know that this vow is a priceless Gift, and you joyfully embrace the great responsibility it represents.

As a student-novice (formally approaching the total practice of the Way of Adidam), you are initiated into formal meditation and sacramental worship, you begin to adapt to a wide range of life-disciplines, and you begin to participate in the life of the cooperative community of Ruchira Avatar Adi Da's devotees. As a student-novice, you engage in an intensive period of study and "consideration" of the Way of Adidam in all of its details. And, as your practice matures, you are given more and more access to the cultural life of the formally acknowledged practitioners of the total practice of Adidam. After a minimum of three to six months of practice as a student-novice, you may apply for formal acknowledgement as a fully practicing member of the second congregation.

If you find that you are steadily and profoundly moved to dedicate your life one-pointedly to Ruchira Avatar Adi Da Samraj and the Process of Real-God-Realization in His Spiritual Company, then, after a demonstration period of exemplary practice as a member of the second congregation, you may apply to practice as a formal renunciate in the first congregation of the Adidam Pan-Communion.

The two formal renunciate orders in the Way of Adidam are the Lay Renunciate Order and the Ruchira Sannyasin Order. The senior of the two orders is the Ruchira Sannyasin Order, which is the senior cultural authority within the gathering of all four congregations of Avatar Adi Da's devotees. The members of the Ruchira Sannyasin Order are the most exemplary formal renunciate practitioners practicing in the ultimate (sixth and seventh) stages of life in the Way of Adidam. The core of the Ruchira Sannyasin Order, and its senior governing members, will, in the future, be those devotees who have Realized Divine Enlightenment. Ruchira Avatar Adi Da Samraj Himself is

the Founding Member of the Ruchira Sannyasin Order, and will, throughout His Lifetime, remain its Senior Member in every respect.

The Ruchira Sannyasin Order is a retreat Order, whose members are legal renunciates. They are supported and protected in their unique Spiritual role by the Lay Renunciate Order, which is a cultural service Order that serves an inspirational and aligning role for all devotees of Avatar Adi Da.

First-congregation devotees have a special role to play in the Way of Adidam. Adi Da Samraj must have unique human Instrumentality—Spiritually Awakened and Divinely Self-Realized devotees—through whom He can continue to do His Divine Transmission Work after His physical Lifetime. No human being, not even one of Avatar Adi Da's Divinely Enlightened devotees, can "succeed" Ruchira Avatar Adi Da Samraj, in the way that, traditionally, a senior devotee often succeeds his or her Spiritual Master.* Avatar Adi Da Samraj is the Complete Incarnation of the Divine Person—He is truly the <u>Completion</u> of all Spiritual lineages in all times and places. Thus, He remains forever the Divine Awakener and Liberator of all beings. His Spiritually Awakened renunciate devotees will <u>collectively</u> function as His Spiritual Instruments, allowing His Blessing-Power to Pervade and Influence the world.

To become a fully practicing devotee of Avatar Adi Da Samraj (in the second congregation, and potentially moving on to the first congregation), call or write one of our regional centers (see p. 191) and sign up for our preliminary course, "The <u>Only</u> Truth That Sets the Heart Free".

---

*Adi Da Samraj has Said that, after His physical (human) Lifetime, there should always be one (and only one) "Murti-Guru" as a Living Link between Him and His devotees. Each successive "Murti-Guru" is to be selected from among those members of the Ruchira Sannyasin Order who have been formally acknowledged as Divinely Enlightened devotees of Adi Da. "Murti-Gurus" do not function as the independent Guru of practitioners of the Way of Adidam. Rather, they are simply Representations of Adi Da's bodily (human) Form, and a means to Commune with Him.

The Adidam Youth Fellowship

Young people (25 and under) are also offered a special form of relationship to Avatar Adi Da—the Adidam Youth Fellowship. The Adidam Youth Fellowship has two membership bodies—friends and practicing members. A friend of the Adidam Youth Fellowship is simply invited into a culture of other young people who want to learn more about Avatar Adi Da Samraj and His Happiness-Realizing Way of Adidam. A formally practicing member of the Adidam Youth Fellowship acknowledges that he or she has found his or her True Heart-Friend and Master in the Person of Avatar Adi Da Samraj, and wishes to enter into a direct, self-surrendering Spiritual relationship with Him as the Means to True Happiness. Practicing members of the Youth Fellowship embrace a series of disciplines that are similar to (but simpler than) the practices engaged by adult members of the second congregation of Adidam. Both friends and members are invited to special retreat events from time to time, where they can associate with other young devotees of Avatar Adi Da.

To become a member of the Adidam Youth Fellowship, or to learn more about this form of relationship to Avatar Adi Da, call or write:

Vision of Mulund Institute (VMI)
10336 Loch Lomond Road, Suite 146
Middletown, CA 95461
PHONE: (707) 928-6932
FAX: (707) 928-5619
E-MAIL: vmi@adidam.org

Become an Advocate of the Way of Adidam

(In the Fourth Congregation of the Adidam Pan-Communion)

The fourth congregation of the Adidam Pan-Communion is for those who are attracted to the life of devotional intimacy with Avatar Adi Da Samraj and are moved to serve His world-Blessing Work, but who are not presently moved or able to take up the full range of disciplines required of members of the first and second congregations. Thus, if you embrace the fourth-congregation practice, you receive Avatar Adi Da's Spiritual Blessings in your life by assuming the most basic level of responsibility as His devotee. The fourth-congregation practice allows you to develop and deepen true devotional intimacy with Avatar Adi Da, but, because it does not involve the full range of disciplines, it always remains a beginning form of the practice of Adidam. If, as a member of the fourth congregation, you are eventually moved to advance beyond the beginning, you are always invited to transition to the second congregation and embrace the total—and, potentially, Divinely Enlightening—practice of the Way of Adidam.

A principal organization within the fourth congregation is the Transnational Society of Advocates of the Adidam Revelation. Advocates are individuals who recognize Ruchira Avatar Adi Da Samraj as a Source of Wisdom and Blessing in their own lives and for the world, and who want to make a practical response. Advocates serve Ruchira Avatar Adi Da's world-Blessing Work by actively serving the dissemination of His Wisdom-Teaching and by actively advocating Him and the Way of Adidam.

When you become an advocate, you make a formal vow of devotion and service to Ruchira Avatar Adi Da Samraj. As described on pp. 174-75, this vow is a profound and eternal commitment to Avatar Adi Da as Your Divine Heart-Master. By taking this vow, you are committing yourself to perform a specific consistent service to Avatar Adi Da and His Blessing Work, and to embrace the fundamental devotional practice that Avatar Adi Da Gives to all His devotees. This is the practice of Ruchira Avatara Bhakti Yoga—devotion to Ruchira Avatar Adi Da Samraj as your Divine Heart-Master. Advocates do the simplest form of this great practice, which Ruchira Avatar Adi Da summarizes as "Invoke Me, Feel Me, Breathe Me, Serve Me".

The advocate vow is also a commitment to make a monthly donation to help support the publication of Avatar Adi Da's supremely precious Wisdom-Literature (as well as publications about Him and the Way of Adidam), as well as paying an annual membership fee that supports the services of the Society of Advocates.

In addition, Advocates offer their services in the form of whatever practical or professional skills they can bring to creatively serve Ruchira Avatar Adi Da and the Way of Adidam.

To become a member of the Transnational Society of Advocates of the Adidam Revelation, call or write one of our regional centers (see p. 191), or e-mail us at:

correspondence@adidam.org

In addition to members of the Transnational Society of Advocates, those who live in traditional cultures around the world are invited to practice as members of the fourth congregation. The opportunity to practice in the fourth congregation is also extended to all those who, because of physical or other functional limitations, are unable to take up the total practice of the Way of Adidam as required in the first and second congregations.

To become a member of the fourth congregation of Adidam, call or write one of our regional centers (see p. 191), or e-mail us at: correspondence@adidam.org.

Serve the Divine World-Teacher
and His World-Blessing Work
via Patronage or Unique Influence

*(The Third Congregation
of the Adidam Pan-Communion)*

We live at a time when the destiny of mankind and of even the planet itself hangs desperately in the balance. The Divine World-Teacher, Ruchira Avatar Adi Da Samraj, has Manifested at this precarious moment in history in order to Reveal the Way of true Liberation from the disease of egoity. It is only That Gift of true Liberation that can reverse the disastrous trends of our time.

It is the sacred responsibility of those who respond to Ruchira Avatar Adi Da to provide the means for His Divine Work to achieve truly great effect in the world. He must be given the practical means to Bless all beings and to Work with His devotees and others responding to Him in all parts of the world, in whatever manner He is spontaneously moved to do so. He must be able to move freely from one part of the world to another. He must be able to establish Hermitages in various parts of the world, where He can Do His silent Work of Blessing, and where He can also Work with His devotees and others who can be of significant help in furthering His Work by receiving them into His physical Company. Ruchira Avatar Adi Da must also be able to gather around Him His most exemplary formal renunciate devotees—and such formal renunciates must be given practical support so that they can be entirely and one-pointedly devoted to serving Ruchira Avatar Adi Da and to living the life of perpetual Spiritual retreat in His physical Company. And the mere fact that Real God is Present in the world must become as widely known as possible, both through the publication and dissemination of books by and about Ruchira Avatar Adi Da and through public advocacy by people of influence.

If you are a man or woman of unique wealth or unique influence in the world, we invite you to serve Ruchira Avatar Adi Da's world-Blessing Work by becoming His patron. Truly, patronage of the Divine World-Teacher, Ruchira Avatar Adi Da Samraj, exceeds all other possible forms of philanthropy. You are literally helping to change the destiny of countless people by helping to support Ruchira Avatar Adi Da in His world-Blessing Work. You make it possible for Ruchira Avatar Adi Da's Divine Influence to reach people who might otherwise never come to know of Him. You make it possible for Him to make fullest use of His own physical Lifetime—the unique bodily Lifetime of Real God, Perfectly Incarnate. To make the choice to serve Avatar Adi Da via your patronage or unique influence is to allow your own life and destiny, and the life and destiny of all of mankind, to be transformed in the most Graceful way possible.

As a member of the third congregation, your relationship to Ruchira Avatar Adi Da is founded on a vow of Ruchira Avatara Bhakti Yoga—a vow of devotion, through which you commit yourself to serve His Work. In the course of your service to Ruchira Avatar Adi Da (and in daily life altogether), you live your vow of devotion by invoking Him, feeling Him, breathing Him, and serving Him (without being expected to engage the full range of disciplines practiced in the first two congregations). At all times, this practice is the means Ruchira Avatar Adi Da has Given for His third-congregation devotees to remain connected to His constant Blessing. In addition, Ruchira Avatar Adi Da has invited, and may continue to invite, members of the third congregation into His physical Company to receive His Divine Blessing.

If you are able to serve Avatar Adi Da Samraj in this crucial way, please contact us at:

Third Congregation Advocacy
12040 North Seigler Road
Middletown, CA 95461
phone number: (707) 928-4800
FAX: (707) 928-4618
e-mail: third_congregation@adidam.org

The Life of a Formally Practicing Devotee of Ruchira Avatar Adi Da Samraj

(in the First or Second Congregation of Adidam)

Everything you do as a devotee of Ruchira Avatar Adi Da Samraj in the first congregation or the second congregation of Adidam is an expression of your heart-response to Him as your Divine Heart-Master. The life of cultivating that response is Ruchira Avatara Bhakti Yoga—or the Real-God-Realizing practice ("Yoga") of devotion ("Bhakti") to the Ruchira Avatar, Adi Da Samraj.

The great practice of Ruchira Avatara Bhakti Yoga necessarily transforms the whole of your life. Every function, every relationship, every action is moved by the impulse of devotional heart-surrender to Adi Da Samraj.

AVATAR ADI DA SAMRAJ: In every moment you must turn the situation of your life into Ruchira Avatara Bhakti Yoga by exercising devotion to Me. There is no moment in any day wherein this is not your Calling. This is what you must do. You must make every moment into this Yoga by using the body, emotion, breath, and attention in self-surrendering devotional Contemplation of Me. All of those four principal faculties must be turned to Me. By constantly turning to Me, you "yoke" yourself to Me, and that practice of linking (or binding, or connecting) to Real God is religion. Religion, or Yoga, is the practice of moving out of the egoic (or separative, or self-contracted) disposition and state into Oneness with That Which is One, Whole, Absolute, All-Inclusive, and Beyond. [December 2, 1993]

As everyone quickly discovers, it is only possible to practice Ruchira Avatara Bhakti Yoga moment to moment when you establish a foundation of supportive self-discipline that enables you to reel in your attention, energy, and feeling from their random wandering. And so Ruchira Avatar Adi Da has Given unique and extraordinarily full Instruction on a complete range of functional, practical, relational, and cultural disciplines for His first-congregation and second-congregation devotees. These disciplines are not methods for attaining Happiness, but are the present-time expression of prior Happiness:

AVATAR ADI DA SAMRAJ: I do not require the discipline of conventional renunciation. Nor do I allow commitment to the karmas of self-indulgence. My devotees serve Me through the humorous discipline of an ordinary pleasurable life. This is the foundation of their practice of the Way of Adidam.

The "ordinary pleasurable life" of which Avatar Adi Da Samraj Speaks is not based on any kind of attempt to achieve immunity from the inevitable wounds of life. Rather, it is based on the always present disposition of True Happiness—the disposition of ego-transcendence through self-surrendering, self-forgetting Contemplation of Ruchira Avatar Adi Da in every moment. Therefore, the "ordinary pleasurable life" of Avatar Adi Da's devotees involves many practices that support and develop the simplicity and clarity of Happiness and self-transcendence. These practices are "ordinary" in the sense that they are not Enlightenment in and of themselves, but they are, rather, the grounds for a simple, mature, pleasurable, and truly human life, devoted to Real-God-Realization.

These practices in the Way of Adidam include cultural disciplines such as morning and evening meditation, devotional chanting and sacramental worship, study-"consideration" of Ruchira Avatar Adi Da's Wisdom-Teaching, formal weekly retreat days, extended weekend retreats every two to three months, an annual meditation retreat of ten days to six weeks. The life of practice also includes the adaptation to a pure and purifying diet, free from toxifying accessories (such as tobacco, alcohol, caffeine, sugar, and processed foods) and animal products (such as meat, dairy products, and eggs).

Meditation is a unique and precious event in the daily life of Avatar Adi Da Samraj's devotees. It offers the opportunity to relinquish outward, body-based attention and to be alone with Adi Da Samraj, allowing yourself to enter more and more into the sphere of His Divine Transmission.

The practice of sacramental worship, or "puja", in the Way of Adidam is the bodily active counter - part to meditation. It is a form of ecstatic worship of Avatar Adi Da Samraj, using a photographic representation of Him and involving devotional chanting and recitations from His Wisdom-Teaching.

You must deal with My Wisdom-Teaching in some form every single day, because a new form of the ego's game appears every single day. You must continually return to My Wisdom-Teaching, confront My Wisdom-Teaching.
                    Avatar Adi Da Samraj

The beginner in Spiritual life must prepare the body-mind by mastering the physical, vital dimension of life before he or she can be ready for truly Spiritual practice. Service is devotion in action, a form of Divine Communion.

Avatar Adi Da Samraj Offers practical disciplines to His devotees in the areas of work and money, diet, exercise, and sexuality. These disciplines are based on His own human experience and an immense process of "consideration" that He engaged face to face with His devotees for more than twenty-five years.

There is also a discipline of daily exercise which includes morning calisthenics and evening Hatha Yoga exercises. There is progressive adaptation to a regenerative discipline of sexuality and sexual energy. And, as a practical foundation for your personal life and the life of the community of practitioners, there is the requirement to maintain yourself in full employment or full-time service, in order to support the obligations of the sacred institution (the Eleutherian Pan-Communion of Adidam) and the cooperative community organization (the Ruchirasala of Adidam).

All of these functional, practical, relational, and cultural disciplines are means whereby your body-mind becomes capable of effectively conducting Ruchira Avatar Adi Da's constant Blessing-Transmission. Therefore, Ruchira Avatar Adi Da has made it clear that, in order to Realize Him with true profundity—and, in particular, to Realize Him most perfectly, to the degree of Divine Enlightenment—it is necessary to be a formally acknowledged member of either the first or the second congregation engaging the total practice of the Way of Adidam.

One of the ways in which Ruchira Avatar Adi Da Communicates His Divine Blessing-Transmission is through sacred places. During the course of His Teaching and Revelation Work, He Empowered three Sanctuaries as His Blessing-Seats. In each of these Sanctuaries—the Mountain Of Attention in northern California, Love-Ananda Mahal in Hawaii, and Adidam Samrajashram in Fiji—Ruchira Avatar Adi Da has Established Himself Spiritually in perpetuity. He has lived and Worked with devotees in all of His Sanctuaries, and has created in each one special holy sites and temples. In particular, Adidam Samrajashram—His Great Island-Hermitage and world-Blessing Seat—is Ruchira Avatar Adi Da's principal Place of Spiritual Work and Transmission, and will remain so forever after His physical Lifetime. Formally acknowledged devotees are invited to go on special retreats at all three Sanctuaries.

The Mountain Of Attention Sanctuary of Adidam

Love-Ananda Mahal

**Adidam Samrajashram
(Naitauba, Fiji)**

Ruchira Avatar Adi Da writes in *Eleutherios (The Only Truth That Sets The Heart Free)*:

I Have Come to Found (and, altogether, to Make Possible) a New (and Truly "Bright") Age of mankind, an Age That will not begin on the basis of the seeking mummery of ego-bondage, but an Age in Which mankind will apply itself, apart from all dilemma and all seeking, to the Inherently Harmonious Event of Real existence (in the Always Already present-time "Bright" Divine Reality That Is the One and Only Reality Itself).

In the brief period of two and a half decades, and in the midst of this "dark" and Godless era, Ruchira Avatar Adi Da has established His unique Spiritual culture. He has created the foundation for an unbroken tradition of Divine Self-Realization arising within a devotional gathering aligned to His fully Enlightened Wisdom, and always receiving and magnifying His Eternal Heart-Transmission. Nothing of the kind has ever existed before.

There are great choices to be made in life, choices that call on the greatest exercise of one's real intelligence and heart-impulse. Every one of us makes critical decisions that determine the course of the rest of our lives—and even our future beyond death.

The moment of discovering the Divine Avatar, Adi Da Samraj, is the greatest of all possible opportunities. It is pure Grace. How can an ordinary life truly compare to a life of living relationship and heart-intimacy with the greatest God-Man Who has ever appeared—the Divine in Person?

Call or write one of our regional centers and sign up for "The Only Truth That Sets the Heart Free", our preliminary course that prepares you to become a fully practicing devotee of Avatar Adi Da Samraj. Or sign up for any of our other classes, correspondence courses, seminars, events, or retreats. Or call to order more books and continue your reading.

Respond now. Do not miss this miraculous opportunity to enter into direct relationship with Real God.

The Eleutherian Pan-Communion of Adidam

AMERICAS
12040 North Seigler Road
Middletown, CA 95461
(800) 524-4941
(707) 928-4936

PACIFIC-ASIA
12 Seibel Road
Henderson
Auckland 1008
New Zealand
64-9-838-9114

AUSTRALIA
P.O. Box 460
Roseville, NSW 2069
Australia
61-2-9416-7951

EUROPE-AFRICA
Annendaalderweg 10
6105 AT Maria Hoop
The Netherlands
31 (0)20 468 1442

THE UNITED KINGDOM
London, England
0181-7317550

FIJI
P.O. Box 4744
Samabula, Suva, Fiji
381-466

E-MAIL: correspondence@adidam.org

We also have centers in the following places. For their phone numbers and addresses, please contact one of the centers listed above or visit our website: **http://www.adidam.org**.

Americas
San Rafael, CA
Los Angeles, CA
Seattle, WA
Denver, CO
Chicago, IL
Framingham, MA (Boston)
Potomac, MD
    (Washington, DC)
Kauai, HI
Quebec, Canada
Vancouver, Canada

Pacific-Asia
Western Australia
Melbourne, Australia

Europe-Africa
Amsterdam, The Netherlands
Berlin, Germany

The Sacred Literature of Ruchira Avatar Adi Da Samraj

Start by reading *The Promised God-Man Is Here*, the astounding story of Avatar Adi Da's Divine Life and Work.

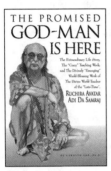

The Promised God-Man Is Here

*The Extraordinary Life-Story,
The "Crazy" Teaching-Work, and
The Divinely "Emerging" World-Blessing
Work Of The Divine World-Teacher
Of The "Late-Time",
Ruchira Avatar Adi Da Samraj,*
by Carolyn Lee, Ph.D.—the profound, heart-rending, humorous, miraculous, wild—and true—story of the Divine Person Alive in human Form. Essential reading as background for the study of Avatar Adi Da's books.

See My Brightness Face to Face

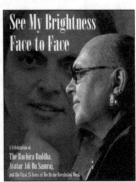

A Celebration of the Ruchira Avatar, Adi Da Samraj, and the First Twenty-Five Years of His Divine Revelation Work—a magnificent year-by-year pictorial celebration of Ruchira Avatar Adi Da's Divine Work with His devotees, from 1972 to 1997. Includes a wealth of selections from His Talks and Writings, numerous Stories of His Divine Work told by His devotees, and over 100 color photographs.

$19.95, 8" x 10" quality paperback, 200 pages

THE FIVE BOOKS OF THE HEART
OF THE ADIDAM REVELATION

After reading *The Promised God-Man Is Here*, continue reading *The Five Books Of The Heart Of The Adidam Revelation*. In these five books, Avatar Adi Da Samraj has distilled the very essence of His Eternal Message to every one, in all times and places.

BOOK ONE:
Aham Da Asmi
(Beloved, I Am Da)

The "Late-Time" Avataric Revelation Of The True and Spiritual Divine Person (The egoless Personal Presence Of Reality and Truth, Which Is The Only Real God)

The most extraordinary statement ever made in human history. Avatar Adi Da Samraj fully Reveals Himself as the Living Divine Person and Proclaims His Infinite and Undying Love for all and All.

$7.95, 4"x7" paperback, 222 pages

BOOK TWO:
Ruchira Avatara Gita
(The Way Of The Divine Heart-Master)

The "Late-Time" Avataric Revelation Of The Great Secret Of The Divinely Self-Revealed Way That Most Perfectly Realizes The True and Spiritual Divine Person (The egoless Personal Presence Of Reality and Truth, Which Is The Only Real God)

Avatar Adi Da Offers to every one the ecstatic practice of devotional relationship to Him—explaining how devotion to a living human Adept-Realizer has always been the source of true religion, and distinguishing true Guru-devotion from cultism.

$7.95, 4"x7" paperback, 254 pages

BOOK THREE:

Da Love-Ananda Gita
(The Free Gift Of The Divine Love-Bliss)

The "Late-Time" Avataric Revelation Of The Great Means To Worship and To Realize The True and Spiritual Divine Person (The egoless Personal Presence Of Reality and Truth, Which Is The Only Real God) Avatar Adi Da Reveals the secret simplicity at the heart of Adidam—relinquishing your preoccupation with yourself (and all your problems and your suffering) and, instead, Contemplating Him, the "Bright" Divine Person of Infinite Love-Bliss.

$7.95, 4"x7" paperback, 234 pages

BOOK FOUR:

Hridaya Rosary
(Four Thorns Of Heart-Instruction)

The "Late-Time" Avataric Revelation Of The Universally Tangible Divine Spiritual Body, Which Is The Supreme Agent Of The Great Means To Worship and To Realize The True and Spiritual Divine Person (The egoless Personal Presence Of Reality and Truth, Which Is The Only Real God)

The ultimate Mysteries of Spiritual life, never before revealed. In breathtakingly beautiful poetry, Avatar Adi Da Samraj sings of the "melting" of the ego in His "Rose Garden of the Heart".

$7.95, 4"x7" paperback, 358 pages

BOOK FIVE:

Eleutherios
(The Only Truth That Sets The Heart Free)

The "Late-Time" Avataric Revelation Of The "Perfect Practice" Of The Great Means To Worship and To Realize The True and Spiritual Divine Person (The egoless Personal Presence Of Reality and Truth, Which Is The Only Real God)

An address to the great human questions about God, Truth, Reality, Happiness, and Freedom. Avatar Adi Da Samraj Reveals how Absolute Divine Freedom is Realized, and makes an impassioned Call to everyone to create a world of true human freedom on Earth.

$7.95, 4"x7" paperback, 270 pages

THE SEVENTEEN COMPANIONS
OF THE TRUE DAWN HORSE

Once you have read *The Five Books Of The Heart Of The Adidam Revelation*, you are ready to continue with *The Seventeen Companions Of The True Dawn Horse*. These seventeen books are "Companions" to *The Dawn Horse Testament*, Avatar Adi Da's great summary of the Way of Adidam (p. 199). Here you will find Avatar Adi Da's Wisdom-Instruction on particular aspects of the true Spiritual Way, and His two tellings of His own Life-Story, as autobiography (*The Knee Of Listening*) and as archetypal parable (*The Mummery*). Avatar Adi Da created the Canon of His Sacred Literature in late 1997 and early 1998, and the Dawn Horse Press is currently in the process of publishing the "Seventeen Companions" and *The Dawn Horse Testament*.

BOOK ONE:
Real God Is The Indivisible Oneness Of Unbroken Light

Reality, Truth, and The "Non-Creator" God
In The True World-Religion Of Adidam

The Nature of Real God and of the cosmos. Why ultimate questions cannot be answered either by conventional religion or by science.

BOOK TWO:
The Truly Human New World-Culture Of Unbroken Real-God-Man

The Eastern Versus The Western Traditional Cultures
Of Mankind, and The Unique New Non-Dual Culture
Of The True World-Religion Of Adidam

The Eastern and Western approaches to religion, and life altogether—and how the Way of Adidam goes beyond this apparent dichotomy.

BOOK THREE:
The Only Complete Way To Realize The Unbroken Light Of Real God

An Introductory Overview Of The "Radical" Divine Way
Of The True World-Religion Of Adidam

The entire course of the Way of Adidam—the unique principles underlying Adidam, and the unique culmination of Adidam in Divine Enlightenment.

BOOK FOUR:

The Knee Of Listening

The Early-Life Ordeal and The "Radical"
Spiritual Realization Of The Ruchira Avatar

Avatar Adi Da's autobiographical account of the years from His
Birth to His Divine Re-Awakening in 1970. Includes a new chapter,
"My Realization of the Great Onlyness of Me, and My Great Regard
for My Adept-Links to the Great Tradition of Mankind".

BOOK FIVE:

The Method Of The Ruchira Avatar

The Divine Way Of Adidam Is An ego-Transcending
Relationship, Not An ego-Centric Technique

Avatar Adi Da's earliest Talks to His devotees, on the fundamental
principles of the devotional relationship to Him and "radical"
understanding of the ego. Accompanied by His summary statement
on His relationship to Swami Muktananda and on His own unique
Teaching and Blessing Work.

BOOK SIX:

The Mummery

A Parable About Finding The Way To My House

A work of astonishing poetry and deeply evocative archetypes. The
story of Raymond Darling's growth to manhood and his search to
be reunited with his beloved, Quandra.

BOOK SEVEN:

He-and-She Is Me

The Indivisibility Of Consciousness and Light
in The Divine Body Of The Ruchira Avatar

One of Avatar Adi Da's most esoteric Revelations—His Primary
"Incarnation" in the Cosmic domain as the "He" of Primal Divine
Sound-Vibration, the "She" of Primal Divine Light, and the "Son" of
"He" and "She" in the "Me" of His Divine Spiritual Body.

BOOK EIGHT:

Divine Spiritual Baptism
Versus Cosmic Spiritual Baptism

Divine Hridaya-Shakti Versus Cosmic Kundalini Shakti
In The Divine Way Of Adidam

The Divine Heart-Power (Hridaya-Shakti) uniquely Transmitted by
Avatar Adi Da Samraj, and how it differs from the various traditional
forms of Spiritual Baptism, particularly Kundalini Yoga.

BOOK THIRTEEN:
What, Where, When, How, Why, and <u>Who</u> To Remember To Be Happy
A Simple Explanation Of The Divine Way Of Adidam
(For Children, and <u>Everyone</u> Else)

A text written specifically for children but inspiring to all—with accompanying Essays and Talks on Divine Ignorance, religious practices for children and young people in the Way of Adidam, and the fundamental practice of whole bodily devotion to Avatar Adi Da Samraj.

BOOK FOURTEEN:
Santosha Adidam
The Essential Summary Of The Divine Way Of Adidam

An extended overview of the entire course of the Way of Adidam, based on the esoteric anatomy of the human being and its correlation to the progressive stages of life.

BOOK FIFTEEN:
The Lion Sutra
The "Perfect Practice" Teachings For Formal Tantric Renunciates In The Divine Way Of Adidam

Practice in the ultimate stages of the Way of Adidam. How the formal renunciate practitioner of Adidam approaches—and passes over—the "Threshold" of Divine Enlightenment.

BOOK SIXTEEN:
The Overnight Revelation Of Conscious Light
The "My House" Discourses On The Indivisible Tantra Of Adidam

Ecstatic Discourses on the Realization and "Practice" of the seventh stage of life. Avatar Adi Da Samraj Describes the primal illusion of egoity—the presumed "difference" between Consciousness and Energy, or Awareness and Love-Bliss—and He Reveals how this illusion is utterly dissolved in the "Open-Eyed" State of the seventh stage of life.

The Basket Of Tolerance

The Perfect Guide To Perfectly <u>Unified</u> Understanding Of The One and Great Tradition Of Mankind, and Of The Divine Way Of Adidam As The Perfect <u>Completing</u> Of The One and Great Tradition Of Mankind

An all-encompassing "map" of mankind's entire history of religious seeking. A combination of a bibliography of over 5,000 items (organized to display Avatar Adi Da's grand Argument relative to the Great Tradition) with over 100 Essays by Avatar Adi Da, illuminating many specific aspects of the Great Tradition.

THE DAWN HORSE TESTAMENT

The Dawn Horse Testament Of The Ruchira Avatar

The "Testament Of Secrets" Of The Divine World-Teacher, Ruchira Avatar Adi Da Samraj

Avatar Adi Da's paramount "Source-Text" which summarizes the entire course of the Way of Adidam. Adi Da Samraj says: "In making this Testament I have been Meditating everyone, contacting everyone, dealing with psychic forces everywhere, in all time. This Testament is an always Living Conversation between Me and absolutely every one."

The Dawn Horse Press

I n addition to Avatar Adi Da's 23 "Source-Texts", the Dawn Horse Press offers hundreds of other publications and items for meditation and sacred worship—courses, videotapes, audiotapes, compact discs, magazines, photos, incense, sacred art and jewelry, and more. Call today for a full catalog of products or visit our website (http://dhp.adidam.org) where you will find full-color images of all our products and on-line ordering.

For more information or a free catalog:
CALL TOLL-FREE 1-800-524-4941
(Outside North America call 707-928-4936)

Visit us on-line at **http://dhp.adidam.org**

Or e-mail: **dhp@adidam.org**

Or write:

THE DAWN HORSE PRESS
12040 North Seigler Road
Middletown, CA 95461 USA

We accept Visa, MasterCard, personal checks, and money orders. In the USA, please add $4.00 (shipping and handling) for the first book and $1.00 for each additional book. California residents add 7.25% sales tax. Outside the USA, please add $7.00 (shipping and handling) for the first book and $3.00 for each additional book. Checks and money orders should be made payable to the Dawn Horse Press.

An Invitation to Support Adidam

Avatar Adi Da Samraj's sole Purpose is to act as a Source of continuous Divine Grace for everyone, everywhere. In that spirit, He is a Free Renunciate and He owns nothing. Those who have made gestures in support of Avatar Adi Da's Work have found that their generosity is returned in many Blessings that are full of His healing, transforming, and Liberating Grace—and those Blessings flow not only directly to them as the beneficiaries of His Work, but to many others, even all others. At the same time, all tangible gifts of support help secure and nurture Avatar Adi Da's Work in necessary and practical ways, again similarly benefiting the entire world. Because all this is so, supporting His Work is the most auspicious form of financial giving, and we happily extend to you an invitation to serve Adidam through your financial support.

You may make a financial contribution in support of the Work of Adi Da Samraj at any time. You may also, if you choose, request that your contribution be used for one or more specific purposes.

If you are moved to help support and develop Adidam Samrajashram (Naitauba), Avatar Adi Da's Great Island-Hermitage and World-Blessing Seat in Fiji, and the circumstance provided there and elsewhere for Avatar Adi Da and the other members of the Ruchira Sannyasin Order, the senior renunciate order of Adidam, you may do so by making your contribution to The Love-Ananda Samrajya, the Australian charitable trust which has central responsibility for these Sacred Treasures of Adidam.

To do this: (1) if you do not pay taxes in the United States, make your check payable directly to "The Love-Ananda Samrajya Pty Ltd" (which serves as the trustee of the Foundation) and mail it to The Love-Ananda Samrajya at P.O. Box 4744, Samabula, Suva, Fiji; and (2) if you do pay taxes in the United States and you would like your contribution to be tax-deductible under U.S. laws, make your check payable to "The

Eleutherian Pan-Communion of Adidam", indicate on your check or accompanying letter that you would like your contribution used for the work of The Love-Ananda Samrajya, and mail your check to the Advocacy Department of Adidam at 12040 North Seigler Road, Middletown, California 95461, USA.

If you are moved to help support and provide for one of the other purposes of Adidam, such as publishing the sacred Literature of Avatar Adi Da, or supporting either of the other two Sanctuaries He has Empowered, or maintaining the Sacred Archives that preserve His recorded Talks and Writings, or publishing audio and video recordings of Avatar Adi Da, you may do so by making your contribution directly to The Eleutherian Pan-Communion of Adidam, specifying the particular purposes you wish to benefit, and mailing your check to the Advocacy Department of Adidam at the above address.

If you would like more information about these and other gifting options, or if you would like assistance in describing or making a contribution, please write to the Advocacy Department of Adidam at the above address or contact the Adidam Legal Department by telephone at (707) 928-4612 or by FAX at (707) 928-4062.

Planned Giving

We also invite you to consider making a planned gift in support of the Work of Avatar Adi Da Samraj. Many have found that through planned giving they can make a far more significant gesture of support than they would otherwise be able to make. Many have also found that by making a planned gift they are able to realize substantial tax advantages.

There are numerous ways to make a planned gift, including making a gift in your Will, or in your life insurance, or in a charitable trust.

If you would like to make a gift in your Will in support of the work of The Love-Ananda Samrajya: (1) if you do not pay taxes in the United States, simply include in your Will the statement, "I give to The Love-Ananda Samrajya Pty Ltd, as trustee of The Love-Ananda Samrajya, an Australian charitable trust, P.O. Box 4744, Samabula, Suva, Fiji, _____" [inserting in the blank the amount or description of your contribution]; and (2) if you do pay taxes in the United States and you would like your contribution to be free of estate taxes and to also reduce any estate taxes payable on the remainder of your estate, simply include in your Will the statement, "I give to The Eleutherian Pan-Communion of Adidam, a California non-profit corporation, 12040 North Seigler Road, Middletown, California 95461, USA, _____" [inserting in the blank the amount or description of your contribution].

To make a gift in your life insurance, simply name as the beneficiary (or one of the beneficiaries) of your life insurance policy the organization of your choice (The Love-Ananda Samrajya or The Eleutherian Pan-Communion of Adidam), according to the foregoing descriptions and addresses. If you are a United States taxpayer, you may receive significant tax benefits if you make a contribution to The Eleutherian Pan-Communion of Adidam through your life insurance.

We also invite you to consider establishing or participating in a charitable trust for the benefit of Adidam. If you are a United States taxpayer, you may find that such a trust will provide you with immediate tax savings and assured income for life, while at the same time enabling you to provide for your family, for your other heirs, and for the Work of Avatar Adi Da as well.

The Advocacy and Legal Departments of Adidam will be happy to provide you with further information about these and other planned gifting options, and happy to provide you or your attorney with assistance in describing or making a planned gift in support of the Work of Avatar Adi Da.

Further Notes to the Reader

An Invitation to Responsibility

A didam, the Way of the Heart that Avatar Adi Da has Revealed, is an invitation to everyone to assume real responsibility for his or her life. As Avatar Adi Da has Said in *The Dawn Horse Testament Of The Ruchira Avatar,* "If any one Is Interested In The Realization Of The Heart, Let him or her First Submit (Formally, and By Heart) To Me, and (Thereby) Commence The Ordeal Of self-Observation, self-Understanding, and self-Transcendence." Therefore, participation in the Way of Adidam requires a real struggle with oneself, and not at all a struggle with Avatar Adi Da, or with others.

All who study the Way of Adidam or take up its practice should remember that they are responding to a Call to become responsible for themselves. They should understand that they, not Avatar Adi Da or others, are responsible for any decision they may make or action they may take in the course of their lives of study or practice. This has always been true, and it is true whatever the individual's involvement in the Way of Adidam, be it as one who studies Avatar Adi Da's Wisdom-Teaching or as a formally acknowledged member of Adidam.

Honoring and Protecting the Sacred Word through Perpetual Copyright

Since ancient times, practitioners of true religion and Spirituality have valued, above all, time spent in the Company of the Sat-Guru (or one who has, to any degree, Realized Real God, Truth, or Reality, and who, thus, Serves the awakening process in others). Such practitioners understand that the Sat-Guru literally Transmits his or her (Realized) State to every one (and every thing) with whom (or with which) he or she comes in contact. Through this Transmission, objects, environments, and rightly prepared individuals with which the Sat-Guru has contact can become Empowered, or Imbued with the Sat-Guru's Transforming Power. It is by this process of Empowerment that things and beings are made truly and literally sacred, and things so sanctified thereafter function as a Source of the Sat-Guru's Blessing for all who understand how to make right and sacred use of them.

Sat-Gurus of any degree of Realization and all that they Empower are, therefore, truly Sacred Treasures, for they help draw the practitioner more quickly into the process of Realization. Cultures of true Wisdom have always understood that such Sacred Treasures are precious (and fragile) Gifts to humanity, and that they should be honored, protected, and reserved for right sacred use. Indeed, the word "sacred" means "set apart", and, thus, protected, from the secular world. Avatar Adi Da has Conformed His body-mind Most Perfectly to the Divine Self, and He is, thus, the most Potent Source of Blessing-Transmission of Real God, or Truth Itself, or Reality Itself. He has for many years Empowered (or made sacred) special places and things, and these now Serve as His Divine Agents, or as literal expressions and extensions of His Blessing-Transmission. Among these Empowered Sacred Treasures is His Wisdom-Teaching, which is Full of His Transforming Power. This Blessed and Blessing Wisdom-Teaching has Mantric Force, or the literal Power to Serve Real-God-Realization in those who are Graced to receive it.

Therefore, Avatar Adi Da's Wisdom-Teaching must be perpetually honored and protected, "set apart" from all possible interference and wrong use. The fellowship of devotees of Avatar Adi Da is committed to the perpetual preservation and right honoring of the sacred Wisdom-Teaching of the Way of Adidam. But it is also true that, in order to fully accomplish this, we must find support in the world-society in which we live and in its laws. Thus, we call for a world-society and for laws that acknowledge the Sacred, and that permanently protect It from insensitive, secular interference and wrong use of any kind. We call for, among other things, a system of law that acknowledges that the Wisdom-Teaching of

206

the Way of Adidam, in all Its forms, is, because of Its sacred nature, protected by perpetual copyright.

We invite others who respect the Sacred to join with us in this call and in working toward its realization. And, even in the meantime, we claim that all copyrights to the Wisdom-Teaching of Avatar Adi Da and the other sacred Literature and recordings of the Way of Adidam are of perpetual duration.

We make this claim on behalf of The Love-Ananda Samrajya Pty Ltd, which, acting as trustee of The Love-Ananda Samrajya, is the holder of all such copyrights.

Avatar Adi Da and the Sacred Treasures of Adidam

True Spiritual Masters have Realized Real God (to one degree or another), and, therefore, they bring great Blessing and introduce Divine Possibility to the world. Such Adept-Realizers Accomplish universal Blessing Work that benefits everything and everyone. They also Work very specifically and intentionally with individuals who approach them as their devotees, and with those places where they reside and to which they Direct their specific Regard for the sake of perpetual Spiritual Empowerment. This was understood in traditional Spiritual cultures, and, therefore, those cultures found ways to honor Adept-Realizers by providing circumstances for them where they were free to do their Spiritual Work without obstruction or interference.

Those who value Avatar Adi Da's Realization and Service have always endeavored to appropriately honor Him in this traditional way by providing a circumstance where He is completely Free to do His Divine Work. Since 1983, He has resided principally on the island of Naitauba, Fiji, also known as Adidam Samrajashram. This island has been set aside by Avatar Adi Da's devotees worldwide as a Place for Him to do His universal Blessing Work for the sake of everyone, as well as His specific Work with those who pilgrimage to Adidam Samrajashram to receive the special Blessing of coming into His physical Company.

Avatar Adi Da is a legal renunciate. He owns nothing and He has no secular or religious institutional function. He Functions only in Freedom. He, and the other members of the Ruchira Sannyasin Order, the senior renunciate order of Adidam, are provided for by The Love-Ananda Samrajya, which also provides for Adidam Samrajashram altogether and ensures the permanent integrity of Avatar Adi Da's Wisdom-Teaching, both in its archival and in its published forms. The Love-Ananda Samrajya, which functions only in Fiji, exists exclusively to provide for these Sacred Treasures of Adidam.

Outside Fiji, the institution which has developed in response to Avatar Adi Da's Wisdom-Teaching and universal Blessing is known as "The Eleutherian Pan-Communion of Adidam". This formal organization is active worldwide in making Avatar Adi Da's Wisdom-Teaching available to all, in offering guidance to all who are moved to respond to His Offering, and in providing for the other Sacred Treasures of Adidam, including the Mountain Of Attention Sanctuary (in California) and Love-Ananda Mahal (in Hawaii). In addition to the central corporate entity known as The Eleutherian Pan-Communion of Adidam, which is based in California, there are numerous regional entities which serve congregations of Avatar Adi Da's devotees in various places throughout the world.

Practitioners of Adidam worldwide have also established numerous community organizations, through which they provide for many of their common and cooperative community needs, including those relating to housing, food, businesses, medical care, schools, and death and dying. By attending to these and all other ordinary human concerns and affairs via self-transcending cooperation and mutual effort, Avatar Adi Da's devotees constantly free their energy and attention, both personally and collectively, for practice of the Way of Adidam and for service to Avatar Adi Da Samraj, to Adidam Samrajashram, to the other Sacred Treasures of Adidam, and to The Eleutherian Pan-Communion of Adidam.

All of the organizations that have evolved in response to Avatar Adi Da Samraj and His Offering are legally separate from one another, and each has its own purpose and function. Avatar Adi Da neither directs, nor bears responsibility for, the activities of these organizations. Again, He Functions only in Freedom. These organizations represent the collective intention of practitioners of Adidam worldwide not only to provide for the Sacred Treasures of Adidam, but also to make Avatar Adi Da's Offering of the Way of Adidam universally available to all.

INDEX

NOTE TO THE READER: Page numbers in **boldface** type refer to the Scriptural Text of *Aham Da Asmi*. All other page numbers refer to the introductions, endnotes, and the back matter.

A

abuses made by egoity, **82**
addresses
   Dawn Horse Press, 168, 201
   e-mail, 166, 178, 183, 191, 201
   regional centers, 166, 191
   Third Congregation Advocacy, 183
   Vision of Mulund Institute, 178
   websites, 168, 169, 191
Adept-Realizer, devotion to, **82**, **83-84**
Adi (Name), 12
Adi, defined, **109**
Adi-Buddha, **97**
   defined, 150
Adidam
   Avatar Adi Da is here to establish, 12
   Avatar Adi Da is the Way of, 34
   described, 33-40, 173-91
   ego-transcending, **71**, **83**, **84**, **87**
   establishment of, 25, 31
   Invitation to formal practice, 171-72
   is free of traditional limitations, 56
   meaning of the name, 34, 160
   as Name of the Way of the Heart, **105**
   and no-seeking, 34-36
   not a struggle, 34
   offers more than traditional Realizations, 36
   as Pleasure Dome, 156
   and "radical" understanding, 20
   as the relationship with Adi Da Samraj, 32
   renunciate orders, 32, 51, 173-77
   and Samadhis, 162
   Secret of, **81**
   and stages of life, 152-55
   taking up the Way of, 47-48
   total practice of the Way of, defined, 52
   undermining of cultism, **73**
   as Way of Communion with Adi Da Samraj, **123**
   as Way of "Radical Understanding", **71**, **83**, 89
   as Way of Real God, **68**, **70**
   as Way of Satsang, **71**
   as Way of the Heart, **71**, **87**

Adidama, defined, 52
Adidama Quandra Mandala, 39-40
   defined, 53
Adidam Pan-Communion, 172-83
Adidam Samrajashram, 32, 189
Adidam Youth Fellowship, 178
Adi Da Samraj
   Adept-Realizer, **83**, **84**
   as Avadhoot, 25-27
   awakening to "radical" understanding, 19-20
   Birth, 12, 15
   Blessing Work, 31-33, **72**, **76**, **81**
   the "Bond" with Him, 38-39, **127**, 162
   books by and about, 167-68, 192-99
   Calling of, **72**, **78-79**, **82**, **83**
   came to "save the world", 45
   Confession of, 62, **70**
   "cracking the cosmic code", 23
   "Crazy" Manner, 25-27, **72**, 151
   "Crazy Wise" manner of, 50-51
   Delighted by His devotees, **128**
   Divine Descent of, **103**
   Divine "Emergence", 28-31, **82**, **87**, 90, **103**, 152
   Divine Giver, **70**, **94**
   Divine Identity of, 9, 13, 22-23, **69-70**, **81-82**, **83**, **86-87**
   Divine Names of, 12-13, 161
   Divine Presence and Person of, **80**, 90
   Divine Re-Awakening of, 21-23
   Divine Siddhis of, 11, **136**
   Divine World-Teacher, **70**, **83**, 90
   early life Ordeal of, 16-17, 20-21
   as Eternally Present and Omni-Present, **132**
   experiences in His Company, 13
   Final Revelation of, **94**
   as First, Last, and Only Adept-Realizer of seventh stage, 37, **83**, **98**
   "forgetting" the "Bright", 16
   Fulfillment of Great Tradition, **84**, 90
   as Great Advantage, **135**
   Gurus of, 17-18

213

215

I do not simply recommend or turn men and women to Truth. I *Am* Truth. I Draw men and women to My Self. I *Am* the Present Real God, Desiring, Loving, and Drawing up My devotees. I have Come to Be Present with My devotees, to Reveal to them the True Nature of life in Real God, which is Love, and of mind in Real God, which is Faith. I Stand always Present in the Place and Form of Real God. I accept the qualities of all who turn to Me, dissolving those qualities in Real God, so that *Only* God becomes the Condition, Destiny, Intelligence, and Work of My devotees. I look for My devotees to acknowledge Me and turn to Me in appropriate ways, surrendering to Me perfectly, depending on Me, full of Me always, with only a face of love.

I am waiting for you. I have been waiting for you eternally.

Where are you?

AVATAR ADI DA SAMRAJ
1 9 7 1